A 1950s Housewife

MARRIAGE AND HOMEMAKING IN THE 1950s

SHEILA HARDY

The History Press

First published 2012
This edition published 2015

The History Press
The Mill, Brimscombe Port
Stroud, Gloucestershire, GL5 2QG
www.thehistorypress.co.uk

British Library Cataloguing in Publication Data.
A catalogue record for this book is available from the British Library.

ISBN 978 0 7509 6414 2

Typesetting and origination by The History Press
Printed and bound in Malta by Melita Press

Contents

Acknowledgements

The author owes a huge debt of gratitude to all those who, with great generosity, honesty and good humour, shared their memories and often their precious mementoes. So must go thanks to: Mesdames Angland, Billsberry, Bolton, Brittain, Coker, Hale, Hepburn, Jacobs, Lankester, Lawrence, Lemon, Perrins, Porter, Randall, Richardson, Slater, Smith, Stannard, Titshall, Watkins and Wheeler. Thank you too, to the Troll family of Cumbria, Pamela Henderson in Wiltshire and Patricia Yelland in Suffolk; valuable contributions also came from the members of the Grundisburgh Lunch Club and the 55 Alive group at the Chantry Library in Ipswich. Sincere thanks too, to the men who became involved in the search: Gordon Bolton and David Bray provided some very useful photographs; David Burnett gave information about the Suffolk chlorophyll industry while John Kirkland happily allowed the author to draw on his wide knowledge of the banking world as well as the magazine collection of his late wife, Monica. The author's sister-in-law Ursula Hardy loaned her a very precious and most helpful copy of *Woman's Weekly,* dating from 1959, while Rachel Field gave practical help and support. Gratitude must also go to the following representatives of the firms owning the copyright of some of the material used here: David Abbott of IPC Media, Colin Raistrick of Proctor & Gamble and Novia Imm of Hoover-Candy. Thank you, each and every one, but especially to the author's loving and long-suffering husband, Michael, who unexpectedly found himself experiencing the life of a housewife during the writing of this book.

Author's Note on Illustrations

All the photographs and items of personal memorabilia herein have been reproduced with the permission of their owners, all of whom have been thanked in the Acknowledgements. However, in respecting those who wished for anonymity, it was decided that only descriptive captions should appear on some illustrations.

Introduction

To someone who spends most of her time researching the lives of those who lived in the eighteenth and nineteenth centuries, the idea that the second half of the twentieth could be classed as history came as a shock. How could the 1950s, a decade from my own life, possibly be looked at in a historical context? I was suddenly confronted with having to heed my own teaching. I had so often cautioned my audiences to beware of sweeping statements and stereotypical pictures of, for example, the Victorian Age, reminding them that Britain in 1837 was a very different place to the country in 1901. How often have I had to hold my peace when a class of children announced they had 'done' the Victorians when in fact all their learning had been focused on a mixed bag of facts about the last twenty years of the reign.

Having recovered from the suggestion that I was now considered part of history, I began to see the advantages of writing about aspects of life in the 1950s. Doing the required research would at least give me a valid reason to bore my grandchildren with stories of what life was like 'when I was a girl'.

In an effort to be as accurate as possible, I enlisted the aid of others and together we set out down memory lane, trying hard not to fall into the trap of talking about the good old days on the one hand and exaggerating how hard life was on the other. We ended up amazed at the changes we have witnessed – not all of them for the better – and we lamented some of the things we had lost, but also gave thanks for the many benefits we have gained. It has done us good to examine our lives in relation to those of our parents' and to look at where we fit into the social history of the twentieth century. I hope this book will be enjoyed by those who can say, 'Oh yes, I remember that!' as well as those who didn't listen, but now wish they had, to the stories their mothers and grandmothers told them. And to the young who may one day be studying the history of Britain during the reign of Elizabeth II, I offer just a small insight into the lives of young women who became housewives in the 1950s.

The girls embarking on married life in the 1950s were products of the two or even three decades earlier. Their parents would have lived through the First World War, and it is likely that some of their fathers emerged from that with both physical and psychological injuries that would have affected their home life. The immediate post-war period of the 1920s is often depicted as a giddy, frivolous time – as it was for a certain class – but for the bulk of the population it was the era of great social unrest that, in the General Strike of 1926, highlighted the wide divide in the British class system. Of much greater impact was the period between 1929 and 1932, when the crash of the stock markets both here and in America had far-reaching economic effects, leading to what became known as the Depression. Unemployment was rife and home life for many was disrupted when fathers were forced to leave temporarily to seek work in other areas. This often left wives and mothers in desperate circumstances, scrimping to pay the rent to keep a roof over the heads of the family, as well as feed and clothe them all. Invariably, in an age when the only way out of a tight situation was to borrow money either by pawning items – father's best suit and mother's wedding ring being the most popular items – or from a loan company that charged high interest, it was not long before the family was forced to seek assistance from the Poor Law Board. Niggardly allowances were often handed out in such a manner that did nothing to help the recipients' 'feeling of self-worth' – a phrase and a concept unheard of at the time.

The 1930s continued to be a time of turmoil with the Abdication Crisis of 1936. Following the death of King George V at the beginning of the year, the Prince of Wales was formally declared his successor, to be known as Edward VIII. The prince had been tremendously popular with the working classes. They felt he understood and sympathised with their plight far better than any politician; to use a phrase, again unheard of at that time, he had charisma, which manifested itself when, for example, he visited striking miners in South Wales or the unemployed in the north. But, although there were rumours, the people knew little of the seriousness of his friendship with the American divorcee, Mrs Wallis Simpson. We had to wait until the twenty-first century and the development of internet channels before the private lives of celebrities became common knowledge. In the 1930s the press and cinema newsreel pictures were discreet, so it came as a shock to a large part of the nation when it became known that the new king wanted to marry Mrs Simpson. It was a shock because it struck at the heart of everything the monarchy stood for. Royalty was expected to marry royalty – a suitable princess from one of the European countries could be found – or, if not, at least a young woman from amongst the English aristocracy. The Church did not recognise the remarriage of a divorcee while the previous partner was still living. Thus, as head of the Church of England, the king could not marry someone who had had not one, but two, previous marriages. At a time when the barriers of class still predominated, the expectation of the majority of the population was that those in authority should set an example and, for most people, even those who did not marry in church, the expectation was that once married they would stay with their partner through thick or thin. When it became necessary for Mrs Simpson to obtain a divorce from Mr Simpson, she discreetly took

Who's this walking down our street? It's Mrs Simpson's bandy feet.

up residence for a short time in the quiet east coast seaside town of Felixstowe (it was out of season), in the hope that her divorce suit might pass unnoticed when it was heard in court in nearby Ipswich. It was rumoured amongst the locals, after the event, that all off-duty policemen were required to fill all the seats in the court, including those normally reserved for the press. True or not, it was certain that children of the town quickly learned to sing: Who's this walking down our street? It's Mrs Simpson's bandy feet She's been married twice before Now she's knocking at Edward's door. Not quite Facebook or Twitter but it spread just as quickly.

Before his Coronation could take place, Edward abdicated (an act almost unknown in British history) and his place was taken by his brother Albert who reigned as George VI and was the father of Queen Elizabeth II. Having survived that storm, and with the country gradually settling down to slow economic growth, outside pressures came with the rise of fascism, particularly on the Continent, with the increased power of Hitler and the

She's been married twice before, now she's knocking at Edward's door.

Nazi Party in Germany, Mussolini in Italy and Franco in Spain. Many idealistic British socialists got their first taste of modern warfare when they went off to fight in the Spanish Civil War of 1938. Then, just four months before the fourth decade of the twentieth century began, Britain declared war on Germany.

Our 1950s bride was at that time coming towards the end of her school days. After six years at primary school, those whose parents could afford it sent their daughters either to a small school for young ladies (reputed to specialise in flower arranging and not much else) or to the fee-paying grammar schools for girls. These schools offered a proportion of free places each year to 11-year-olds who passed the Scholarship, an examination taken in two parts. The written papers were taken in the pupils' primary school but the oral part, which was taken only by those who had passed the written exams, took place at the grammar school. It lasted for most of the day, the candidates attending lessons, having lunch and finally enduring an interview with the headmistress. It was rumoured that this weeded out those with poor manners, particularly at the table! Once accepted, the girls and their

A 1950s housewife baking. *Mary Evans / Classic Stock / H. Armstrong Roberts*

classmates would have enjoyed an academic education leading to the School Certificate, taken at 16. Those girls who were considered clever and aspired to enter one of the professions – mainly teaching at this time – stayed on to take the Higher School Certificate. The option, apart from nursing, for those who left at 16 seemed to be mainly in secretarial work, so often a year followed learning shorthand and typing to the required speeds at either a Pitman's or private secretarial college.

For the rest of the female population, in towns they progressed to central or municipal secondary schools at 11 where they had a watered down version of the grammar school curriculum, but one that was preparing them for work in shops and offices when they left school at 14. In country areas, pupils might stay at the same school for their whole school career and the curriculum there was heavily biased to the idea that the girls coming from an agricultural background would continue in it after marriage. At least by this time domestic service was no longer the main career path for girls. Those with skills such as dressmaking were in demand in factories, while those entirely unskilled could still find work that suited them.

But then it all changed. The declaration of war in September 1939 brought major upheaval on many fronts and hurtled our future 1950s bride along unforeseen paths. Those still at school might have found themselves evacuated with their schools to different parts of the country. City girls found themselves among unfamiliar rural landscapes. Families were broken up and new ties, some very long lasting, were forged with strangers from very different walks of life. Career plans for some might have to be put on hold, while for others the war brought opportunities of which they had never dreamed. For many there was the option to join one of the women's branches of the army, navy or air force, bringing with it the opportunity to learn such skills as driving, mechanical engineering or plotting the movements of aircraft. Girls whose educational standard would previously have prevented them from becoming nurses, found that hospitals were happy to admit them as probationers, while older girls found themselves being

'directed' into war work in munitions factories, and into agriculture to replace those young male farm workers who had either enlisted or been called up for service. As more men were released to the services, so more young women began to do work that had once been the preserve of the male population. The female 'clippie', as the replacement of the male bus conductor became known, was one thing, but there were those who thought it a step too far when a 'slip of a girl' was seen at the wheel of a double-decker trolley bus.

Alongside the great change in a girl's working life during the 1940s came the unexpected freedom of her social life. The pre-war girl would have met boys of her own age most probably from amongst her own social circle. The middle-class girl would have been a member of the tennis club and would have joined in all the other social functions that the club provided, while her less well-off friend would have relied on meeting a boyfriend either through work, a mutual friend or at the local dance hall. The parents of the pre-war girl would have probably known the family of

any boy she met and would have been careful to vet their daughter's friends. But everything was different now. Girls who would have lived at home until their marriage were now often living miles away from parental supervision and many were having the time of their lives. Young men in uniform were very attractive, and in their off-duty time looked for female companionship. So it was, that girls from the 1940s onwards found themselves future husbands from not only all over the United Kingdom but also from the United States, Canada, Australia and New Zealand as well as Europe – plain Miss Smith or Jones could have found herself becoming Mrs Unpronounceable.

So our 1950s brides entered the post-war period shaped by what had gone before. For the older ones, having had more freedom their horizons were much wider than those of their parents and their expectations of life were greater. The younger ones, in contrast, had been subjected to a much tighter discipline from home and school. It is said that theirs was the last generation to obey orders without question. Yet like the generations of women who had preceded them, they were about to take the biggest risk of their lives, that of committing themselves to becoming a wife and possibly a mother. We shall find out how some of them coped with this challenge.

1

Going Out

In the 1950s young men and women 'went out' together. Embarrassing uncles were likely to ask, in the sort of whisper that was audible to everyone else sitting round the Sunday tea table, if you were 'courting' yet. Auntie would look coy before saying she was sure it wouldn't be long before you found yourself a nice young man. Like as not, your mother, as she poured tea into the best china cups that came out of the glass cabinet only when you had visitors, as well as at Christmas and for funerals, would assert firmly that there was plenty of time for that sort of nonsense! And the company would all nod in agreement as they worked their way through a salad with ham or even a precious tin of red salmon, followed by pineapple chunks accompanied by a dollop of thick cream from a tin or evaporated milk (both decanted, of course, into a small glass bowl or a jug).

But was there time? For a girl in the 1950s there was still great pressure to find herself a husband. It was expected, or at least accepted, that she would find a 'nice' young man, marry in her early 20s, have children and be a grandmother by her mid-40s. Any young woman who reached the age of 30 without being married or engaged was regarded as being 'on the shelf', soon to be labelled as one of life's spinsters. And the mother who had been certain that there was plenty of time had to start finding excuses for her daughter's lack of matrimonial prospects. Onlookers wondered what was wrong with her: why didn't she catch a man like all her friends? The unattached female who could claim that she was far too busy pursuing a career was fortunate. That is, until her peers let her down by having a career and a husband!

So where did the 1950s girl find her man? In the early part of the decade single-sex secondary schools were the norm, certainly in towns. Traditionally, from the days of the introduction of compulsory education in 1870, the sexes had been taught in separate classes even if in the same building. There were also different playgrounds for each group to make sure there was no fraternising during school hours. Even the 1930s wave of new buildings for grammar and senior schools tended to be just for one sex, frequently situated on sites at a distance from each other. However, teenage boys and girls met as they made their way to and from school; the establishment might segregate the sexes but the local bus service didn't, and many a romance began at the bus stop. Boys soon got to know which routes, whether on foot or bicycle, were followed by the object of their interest. Once a friendship had begun, it was not long before the pair was deemed to be 'going out'.

The second most popular place for young people to meet was through attendance at church or chapel. During the 1940s most young children were sent to Sunday School as a matter of course and well-organised churches made sure that their 'young adolescents' did not drop their attendance by offering other activities during the week. A Bible class for example, a youth choir perhaps, or membership of the affiliated Scouts and Guides or the Nonconformist Boys' and Girls' Brigade. How many young men wearing that neat little cap at a jaunty angle had set a girl's heart on fire as they marched to chapel through the streets on a Sunday morning, blowing a cornet or banging a drum? One had to admit that in the attraction stakes, the Boys' Brigade uniform beat the Scouts' hands down! So, romance often blossomed through the church and this, of course, was an advantage because the parents of the couple would already know each other, at least slightly, and the respective mothers could be content that their son or daughter was 'going out' with someone 'nice and respectable'. Ah, 'respectable', how often we heard that word in the 1950s!

In 1947 the school-leaving age was raised from 14 to 15 for most pupils. However, those in grammar schools were expected to stay until they were 16 in order to sit the School Certificate or Matric, as it was known. Their parents had to sign a bond, which carried a forfeit of £10 (more than a week's wages) if it was broken, agreeing to this extra year. Doing well in the exam meant you could leave and enter certain professions; alternatively it qualified

'It will be a waste of time, she'll only get married'

you to enter the sixth form to study for the Higher School Certificate, which in turn could lead to university or college entry. There was a strong feeling among many parents at the time that it was most important for their sons to receive the very best education they could get, while many bright girls were denied the opportunity to stay on into the sixth form and go further. 'It will be a waste of time, she'll only get married' was often to be heard when discussing a schoolgirl's future. So they, like the majority of the 15-year-olds from the senior schools that had now become secondary moderns, had to find a job.

Once she was out to work, then 1950s woman was free to enjoy a social life. This was most likely to include dancing. During the wartime period of the 1940s dance halls had flourished throughout the country and had provided a pleasant and innocuous pastime for troops billeted away from home. Saturday night dances were held in village halls, school and church halls, right up to the commercially run Lyceums and Mecca ballrooms. Girls usually went with their best friend to enjoy the music and to practise the dance steps they had learned at school or at home from the wireless. Some even got as far as the tango! But there was a problem. If you practised with your friend and you were taller than she was, then you got landed with taking the man's part. This could make for confusion when you got to a proper dance and a young man asked you to dance.

Once inside the hall, having paid the 1s entry fee, and the 3d to leave your coat in the cloakroom the girls tended to sit or stand together while the young men congregated at the other end of the room, thus creating something of a male mini-stampede when the music started. This was the moment when some girls stared into space, hoping and praying that they wouldn't be left unpartnered, while the more blasé decided to be picky in their choice. Throughout the evening a live band played traditional ballroom dances, interspersed with the dreaded Paul Jones, supposed to be a bit of an icebreaker by mixing folk up, but a nightmare for some who were suddenly faced with Mr Flatfoot, Mr Toecrusher or worst of all Mr Breathedown-your-ear as a partner. For the truly energetic – and if you were fortunate with your band – there would also be a chance to jive.

What everyone was really waiting for was the last waltz signalling the end of the evening and the moment many young men had been waiting for. Having decided early on which young woman had caught his eye, he would make sure that he partnered her for the last waltz and, as the lights dimmed and they slowly circled the floor, he would ask if he could see her home. If she liked the look of him she would agree, if not she would come up with an excuse to extricate herself. They would stroll leisurely back to her house together and when they reached her front door he might suggest they meet again. With a chaste kiss, he would

> . . . it was easy to make
> friends with a colleague
> who might one day become
> one's husband.

leave, just before her father or mother would conveniently come to put out the milk bottles on the doorstep.

The workplace offered another popular way to meet a future husband. From offices to factories to department stores, all with a large number of employees, it was easy to make friends with a colleague who might one day become one's husband. For some people a more preferable way of meeting a suitable soulmate was through a social function such as a friend's wedding, a cocktail party or a dance at the Young Farmers' Club, the tennis club or the youth wing of one of the political parties. From the parents' point of view this was much more satisfactory than having your daughter 'picked-up' by a stranger whom she met somewhere by chance. The prime concern of parents was that any future son-in-law should have a good steady job with at least the prospect of a decent income and so be in a position to provide their daughter with a comfortable home. If they were honest, most mothers hoped that their daughter would eventually settle near them, as they themselves had settled near theirs – meaning that they would be on hand to help when necessary. But the war had changed that.

A great many girls fell in love with servicemen . . .

A great many girls fell in love with servicemen who came from different parts of the country, and who expected their wives to eventually go with them to their native area. We must not forget that there were still a great many servicemen around in the 1950s, as every able-bodied young man was expected to do two years of National Service in one of the three armed services. There were also still large numbers of American personnel in air bases all around the country. Most of the girls marrying them found that they would ultimately follow the GI brides of the late 1940s who had sailed the Atlantic to that vast continent, and discover for themselves that it was not necessarily the same as it appeared on the cinema screen. Some married German or Italian prisoners of war and often had to face strong prejudice from both their families and neighbours. Post-war, many Polish ex-servicemen chose to remain in England, as did those from Hungary who were drafted in to undertake the very dangerous task of clearing mines from the beaches of Britain's coastal areas. Girls who married these men were not subjected to criticism, especially as often they had met them through social activities at the local Roman Catholic church. But it has to be said that there was a very strong colour prejudice in the 1950s. Girls who were brave enough to date a black American serviceman were often ostracised by their communities, never mind their parents, and matters did not improve when migrants from the Caribbean arrived.

So, our 1950s girl has been going out with her man for some time and at last he has plucked up the courage to ask her to marry him – or at least decided he loves her enough to want to spend the rest of his life with her. She has probably dropped enough hints that what she wants is marriage. (To be brutally frank, in the 1950s that was the only way a couple were going to enjoy a sex life, but more about that later in the book.) Once the pair had established that marriage was what they both wanted, the young man sought out an opportunity to ask the girl's parents or guardian for their permission. One rarely heard of the request being refused; if it was, then it was likely that, provided the girl was over the age of consent, the couple would go ahead anyway. That would probably have involved a family rift, the girl leaving home and missing out on all the preparations involved in the period up to the wedding.

The woman who had followed the conventional path was now proudly displaying her lovely new engagement ring. (Well, it might be new to her but bearing in mind the cost involved in the purchase, some girls were quite happy to accept a second-hand one.) Quite often the couple chose the ring together and were frequently seen on a Saturday afternoon, hand in hand, gazing into the windows of H. Samuel, the affordable jewellers, where it was possible in 1950 to buy a three-diamond ring from their secondhand range for £25.

The now-extinct Woolworths was an option for those with little money as here it was possible to choose from a wide selection of rings, which included the all-important wedding band. Many a young girl would have tried on a Woolies ring in order to decide which style would best suit her hand when the time came. And when it did, if she did settle for a 'fashion' ring, she was promised that it would be replaced with the real thing when the couple's economic situation improved. With luck that would be before the 'gold' had tarnished. As in everything else, fashion dictated the current designs for rings, with new shapes chosen for the setting of the jewel. The solitaire diamond remained a favourite for many, but others opted for rubies, sapphires and emeralds, all of which had imitation versions, while the more daring went for unusual stones, perhaps one associated with a birthstone. Brave indeed was the girl who chose either an opal or a pearl. If she had a superstitious mother she would be warned that the gift of an opal indicated a changeable nature, while the pearl was said to bring tears. A sharp intake of breath from mother and the marriage was doomed before it started!

2

Something New, Something Borrowed ...

During the period between the engagement and the wedding, saving became the watchword for most couples. This often meant that they severely curtailed their social life, twiceweekly visits to the cinema were cut to one and even that might have to alternate with the Saturday night dance. With both of them still living at home, they were expected to follow the family's house rules, going home after work for their evening meal before meeting up. Most parents expected their sons and daughters, engaged or not, to be home by half past ten at the latest during the week. In those days most cinema performances ended just after ten o'clock and if one was dependent on public transport the last trolley bus or tram was likely to be not many minutes after that. The closeness of the end of a film and the last bus meant leaving the cinema as quickly possible to secure a place in the bus queue, but to do that you had to get out before having to stand for the National Anthem. The whole of the first verse was played and people who dared to walk out before it had finished were severely frowned upon. If you missed the bus, then it meant a long walk home and possibly an irate parent waiting when you got there. Girls rarely had a key to let themselves in but the parents of young men were somewhat more tolerant in allowing that after their son had taken his fiancée home, he was bound to be home closer to eleven o'clock. A concession was made if it was known that the couple was going to a Saturday dance which, by law, had to finish at midnight.

Occasionally, instead of going out, the couple would stay in during the evening, most often at the girl's home where they might be offered the chance to sit in the 'front room', 'parlour'. This room was usually used only on Sundays, when you had visitors or at Christmas time, and in those days before central heating became the norm it was rarely heated except for special occasions. A single bar of the electric fire might be turned on if it was chilly, but parents were likely to remind you about the cost of electricity. In the depth of winter when snow was on the ground, mother might take a shovelful of burning coals from the fire in the living room and transfer it to the grate in the front room. When that had died down almost to ash, it was time for the young man to go home.

The problem with staying in was that one could be plagued by younger members of the family, worst being the giggly little sister who stood in the hall listening for times when the conversation stopped, a sure sign the couple was kissing.

While the pair were busy saving what they could from their weekly wages, the girl started collecting for her 'bottom drawer'. This was a hangover from the distant past when part of a bride's dowry took the form of her coming to the marriage with bed and table linen, cutlery and china

Many girls learned how to 'make do and mend'

sufficient to equip the new home. By Victorian times this had been expanded to what became known as a 'trousseau' and included the bride's wedding dress and other clothes. In some cases all these items were carefully stored in the wooden box familiarly known as a hope chest.

The average working girl in the 1950s could not expect her parents to lay up a store of bed linen, even if they could afford it, for at the beginning of the decade such items were still in short supply, having only been taken off rationing in 1947. Many girls learned how to 'make do and mend' as they watched or helped their mothers put 'sides to middle'. Since cotton sheets receive most of their wear in the middle, after years of use plus the constant boiling in water, they were in danger of becoming so threadbare they would disintegrate into holes. Once a sheet was beyond the stage where it could be patched or darned, both of which could prove to feel scratchy to the skin, then more drastic measures were required. The sheet was cut in half longways and the two outer edges were machined together with a 'run and fell' seam which guaranteed that it would hold together firmly. Unfortunately, the good economic housewife did

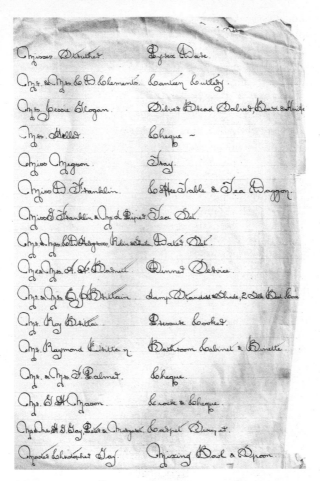

A bridegroom carefully recorded gifts.

not always take into account the fact that trying to sleep on this seam was very uncomfortable, especially if the sheets were made of heavy cotton. Once turned, the new edges were trimmed and then carefully hemmed to prevent fraying.

But what did our 1950s bride put in her 'bottom drawer'? A Saturday afternoon shopping trip in town with her best girlfriend gave her the chance to look for the more mundane items necessary in her new home. Woolworths was the ideal place to search for reasonably priced items; while her mother would have always mashed potatoes with a dinner fork, our 1950s bride could buy a masher plus a couple of other items for which she had yet to discover a use. Woolworths also did a very nice line in china and glassware, so she bought things that took her fancy, knowing that she would be able to go back later to complete the set. The larger department stores, old established family businesses whose names they bore, also provided a happy

Back in the 1950s most people married in church . . .

hunting ground for our future bride. It was here that the bride may have looked at the limited range of bridal wear on offer, deciding what style of dress she would wear for her big day. She might also go into one of the smaller shops that sold ladies' clothing. Here there were specific areas devoted to coats, dresses and formal wear, which included a very small selection of evening gowns, lingerie, hats and gloves. The problem with these shops was that you couldn't just browse and then blatantly walk out, you were expected at least to try something on – and make a purchase – and it was very difficult to avoid the firm but civil assistant who wanted to know the moment you walked in what exactly it was Madam was looking for.

Back in the 1950s most people married in church. This didn't necessarily mean the couple were both regular churchgoers, though their parents often were, but apart from the Registrar's Office, the only people licensed to perform marriages were priests of the Church of England, and unless one received special dispensation the marriage could only take place in the parish church of one of the couple, most usually the bride. Of course it was quite possible for a couple who were Nonconformists or of another religious faith to marry in their particular place of worship, provided that the Registrar's Office was properly informed beforehand. In these cases, a registrar came to the ceremony, supervised the signing of the register and issued the official marriage certificate. Those wishing to have a simpler, civil ceremony often opted to go to the Registry Office itself. These included those couples in which one party was divorced, since they could not be married in a church anyway. Sometimes too, if the bride-to-be had been widowed, it was felt to be more appropriate for her second wedding to be a quiet one – and of course she certainly could not appear in a white wedding gown!

So, back to that all-important dress. Bearing in mind that austerity still lingered, many brides took the option of borrowing a dress. This might even be her mother's, although the 1920s wedding dress did not suit the fashion of the time – oddly enough by the end of the 1950s the length would have been right, if not much else. So better to forget mum's dress and borrow from a recently married friend or relation and placate mum by asking if you could borrow her veil and headdress instead. The second option was to have a dress made. If mother was good with her needle and sewing machine then she would make it. Few homes from the 1930s and '40s were complete without a Singer sewing machine, whether it be grandma's treadle one or the hand-driven portable one. Mother or even the bride herself might make not only the dress but those for the bridesmaids and outfits for the pageboys too. There were several advantages to this apart from the cost, it being much cheaper to make than buy; mother and daughter could pore over patterns and material samples together and the final result would be unique, even if a Simplicity or Butterick pattern had inspired it. The dresses would also fit their wearers perfectly, and colours and materials would all match. If she was no home dressmaker, then the bride had the option of having the dress (or dresses) made by a professional.

Every town, and village too, had ladies, often widowed with a family to support, who had set up businesses in their own home. These clever seamstresses were able to look at pictures in a magazine or pattern book and put the neckline of one on to the bodice of another and join that to the skirt of a third. The bride would buy the material of her choice and her gown would be made up for her at a fraction of the cost of a bought one. When it came to buying dresses, unless the bride and her family could afford it, it was tactfully suggested that the bridesmaids should pay for their own. If this was the case, then the bride needed to be even more tactful in suggesting what she would like them to wear. If the bridesmaid was thinking her dress could double as an evening dress later, then she

was unlikely to want an unusual colour or material. Most brides played it safe by opting to have their attendants in pink, blue or yellow – rarely green as that was considered an unlucky colour. But, as we all know, there are many shades within a colour and so, for example, the bridesmaid cousins who lived miles apart might well turn up for duty in anything from aquamarine and turquoise to dusty pink or deep rose. Taffeta and crepe were the materials much in vogue in the first half of the decade. In the latter years of the 1950s, with the growth in manufacturing and the introduction of new materials, alongside an easing of the economic situation and the influence of America through the cinema, fashion was changing. Fewer brides chose the traditional full-length figured brocade gown with a small train, opting instead for the ballerina-style dress à la Audrey Hepburn. For summer brides, both floral organdie and broderie anglaise were popular, as were layers of tulle over stiffened net petticoats. There was a much more modern feel now to weddings. Gone were the very large bouquets such as Princess Elizabeth had for her wedding. More often than not these had been the virginal white lily or dramatic red carnations or roses with lots of trailing maidenhair fern, while in autumn bronze chrysanthemums were a popular choice, as they also were for funeral wreaths. These were now supplanted by neat posies of more delicate flowers such as tiny pink rosebuds with lily of the valley.

The venue for the wedding breakfast in the early 1950s was most likely to be in a local hall. In those far-off days when hardly anyone had a car, it was essential that the hall should be as close as possible to the church so that guests could comfortably stroll to it after the service. Also popular was the function room upstairs in a convenient public

The biggest drawback, aesthetically speaking, was the overriding smell of beer . . .

house. All these tended to be very basic in their design: walls whitewashed or painted dark green or brown, floors dusty wooden boards or covered with prewar patterned lino, faded with time and wear. The biggest drawback, aesthetically speaking, was the overriding smell of beer and the thick coating of nicotine on the ceiling. But somehow, none of this was a real drawback. A vase or two of flowers, perhaps some coloured crêpe paper streamers across the ceiling, would soon brighten the place up.

Much more important was what food was going to be served. It has to be remembered that rationing of some foods was in operation until as late as 1954. Although tinned and dried fruit, chocolate biscuits, black treacle and golden syrup as well as jellies and mincemeat were de-rationed in 1950, this did not mean that they were all immediately available. Thus, although a 1950s bride would have the dried fruit needed to make the wedding cake and flour, which had been off ration for two years, the other basic ingredients of butter (including margarine), sugar and eggs were still subject to rationing until 1953. Tea had been decontrolled the previous year but meat, bacon and cheese had to wait until 1954. The one saving grace for those catering for a wedding was that they were allowed up to 2lb of ham – so no prizes for guessing what featured on many a wedding menu. Mothers relied on a close network of friends and relations for help with the provision and preparation of the food. Donations of essential ingredients for the baking; precious tins of peaches that had been carefully hoarded for an emergency; fresh cream and eggs; even a chicken or two from farming relations to eke out the ubiquitous ham; fresh vegetables and the essential lettuces and tomatoes from friendly allotment holders – all gifts were most gratefully received. This type of 1950s wedding reception certainly lacked uniformity. There was little concern about co-ordination, colour or otherwise, whether it be for the china and cutlery, which was borrowed, or portion control. The different ladies who made the trifles supplied the dish in which it was served and followed their own particular methods. Hence some could be heavily weighted with sponge cake and little fruit, while others had a thick layer of jelly under the custard and they didn't

> Most weddings took place in the early afternoon, so that gave mother and her helpers the morning to prepare the feast.

all have a fresh cream topping. It was customary for the bride's mother, once the food had all been assembled and the tables laid, to secure the best-looking trifle for the bridal party at the top table.

Most weddings took place in the early afternoon, so that gave mother and her helpers the morning to prepare the feast. Trestle tables were set out as three sides of a square and covered with a number of borrowed white tablecloths with the occasional sheet to make up any deficiency. A vase or two of flowers down the centre of the table and then mismatched cutlery, a plate and a wine glass marked each place, complemented by a carefully handwritten (or typed if the bride worked in an office) card bearing a guest's name. Just as today, hours had been spent deciding who should sit next to whom. In those early days, the meal tended to consist of a main course – meat and vegetables or salad – followed by a dessert (or 'afters') such as the aforementioned trifle, tinned fruit, apple pie and custard. If it was a winter wedding, then soup might be served and a hot baked potato added to the plate of cold meats. There would have been wine – Sauterne was very popular – and

. . . most couples ended up with at least three toast racks . . .

orange squash for the young and abstainers. Speeches and toasts were made, then came the cutting of the cake, one or two tiers of a rich fruit mixture covered in white icing with a simple piped decoration. Small slices of cake were then served along with cups of tea – coffee drinking was still very much in its infancy in the provinces before the mid-1950s.

Modern wedding lists does do away with duplication, but in the '50s it was a perennial joke that most couples ended up with at least three toast racks or, later on, a couple of electric toasters. What most couples needed were the basic essentials: sheets, pillowcases, blankets, an eiderdown (if one was lucky enough to have a wealthy relation), towels and tablecloths, cutlery, a clock, saucepans and dishes – particularly Pyrex as the decade wore on. However, they were actually likely to end up with several sets of silver-plated fish eaters, delicate plated dessert spoons, cake forks and coffee spoons embellished with a coloured

representation of a coffee bean at the end of their fragile handles, all still in their original imitation leather boxes. All these dated from the 1930s or earlier when they had been received as wedding presents by now elderly relations. Unused and unwanted they were handed on. We call it recycling. Much of it is now valuable, so the 1950s bride may regret that, finding it not to her taste, she passed it on to another couple when a shortage of money meant she could ill afford to buy them a gift.

Sometimes, when the hall was close enough to the bride's home, guests would be invited there to see the display of gifts, all neatly arranged with the donors' cards bearing their names beside each one. Having viewed and discussed the presents, for some the wedding reception was now over. Only close family and friends were likely to stay on, for many had buses or trains to catch to distant destinations or young children to collect from whoever had looked after them for the afternoon. The bride and groom also disappeared, and while the remaining guests chatted, perhaps over another drink, the newlyweds went home to change into their going-away outfits, ready to set off for their honeymoon. The new husband might actually keep on the suit he had been wearing but if he was a serviceman and had married in his uniform – that always looked good in the photographs – then he would change into a suit. The bride's outfit was always chosen with great care for it was expected to last her for a year or two, so if it was winter, she would choose a stylish winter coat and a pretty dress or skirt and blouse, with matching shoes and handbag as well as, of course, gloves and a hat. Another good standby was what was known

A wedding in 1957 with a modern 'ballerina-style' dress.

then as a costume but now as a suit; a good tailored affair, preferably in the latest fashion, as it had to last. This too would be completed by, as the local newspaper report of the wedding would have it, 'the matching accessories'.

The bridal pair would then re-emerge in the hall to say their farewells. Someone would have found a car to drive them to the station to catch their train. Suitably

Moving slightly up the social scale would have been a sit-down meal . . .

beribboned at the front and with an old boot and a couple of tin cans trailing from the back, the car carried them off amongst the cheers of well-wishers, but not before the bride had thrown her bouquet behind her towards the anxiously waiting young females who hoped they might be next.

Obviously, much of the foregoing is full of generalities as no two weddings were ever exactly the same. Much depended on the financial circumstances of the family. Since it was customary for the father of the bride to pay for the reception as well as other expenses – and there were little books of rather outdated etiquette which explained who paid for what – if he had sufficient savings for this day, the whole thing would have been different. Moving slightly up the social scale would have been the sit-down meal of three courses in a local restaurant or hotel, with the cake ordered from a professional baker. In 1956 it was possible to have such a reception for thirty guests for £50. It would have been a bit more formal than the one described earlier, but again, all over within the afternoon. An alternative to this was the sort of affair which involved

Happy Wedding Day: a 1950s card showing the bride arriving at the church with her two bridesmaids, while a pageboy reaches up to ring the bells. *Mary Evans Picture Library/GILL STOKER*

standing around with nothing more than a glass or two of champagne and a selection of canapés – a terrible disappointment for guests who had travelled halfway across the country by train, had eaten nothing since breakfast, and could not afford the dining car on the return journey. Never would a bag of chips have tasted so good, even if the chip shop owner would have been somewhat taken aback by the arrival of floral-hatted and white-gloved customers. Those who had the space and money were able to hold the reception in a marquee in their garden. Responsibility for the smooth running devolved upon the outside caterers who not only saw to the delivery of the gold- or white-painted chairs and circular tables to hold eight or ten guests each, but also dealt with all the food, providing the staff to serve the meal and wine. Florists would also have been in attendance either the day before or on the morning of the wedding. The whole operation would have been carried out with almost military-style precision, with a master of ceremonies directing who should make the speeches and when.

Throughout the meal music would have been provided, perhaps by a string quartet or a solo harpist. To guard against misfortunes such as heavy rain, high winds or deep snow, the wedding party would go to the photographer's studio on leaving the church, and there a simple series of formal portraits such as the bride and groom alone – to be reproduced in cabinet size for both sets of parents to frame and hang on the sitting room wall or stand on top of the piano – the bride, groom, their parents, the best man and the bridesmaids, in a smaller size and given to those involved and close relations, would be taken. If money was no object then an album was also purchased. The professional might also attend at the church to take going-in and coming-out pictures, but on no account would he be allowed to disturb the service with his camera.

There were those receptions, usually held in late after-noon, where, following the meal, cake cutting and so forth, there would be a period when the guests would leave the tables and mingle while the newlyweds would circulate throughout the room talking to as many of the guests as possible. For some this was the time to slip away, for others it was a chance to light up their cigarettes or for some men a chance to visit the bar for a beer. The women tended to make for the 'Ladies', to repair their make-up and discuss their true opinion about the whole proceedings so far. Once the tables had been cleared it was time for the dancing to begin, with the bride and groom circling the floor several times on their own – an embarrassing time for some. Music might be provided by a small three-piece band or simply a friend with a record player and a collection of 78 and 45 records.

> . . . in 1957 a fortnight's package holiday by air to the Italian Riviera cost about £30 per person.

Like so many things during the decade, the honeymoon was shaped by whether it took place before or after 1956. Those who honeymooned after that date had options that would have seemed unbelievable in 1950. They could, if they wished, go abroad, not just by ferry boat to France and then on by train to places in Europe like Austria, but on two-week package holidays by air offered by newly set up holiday companies. This was indeed an exciting prospect.

At popular times of the year, these holiday flights could be filled almost entirely with the recently married, especially those who had married before 5 April, as this allowed a bridegroom to claim the married man's allowance for the whole of the previous tax year, bringing him a substantial tax rebate. On the subject of money, in 1957 a fortnight's package holiday by air to the Italian Riviera cost about £30 per person. This took some saving and, of course, there was also the need to have some spending money for incidentals like drinks and ice creams. Fortunately, the amount you had available to spend while you were away was limited not just by your own personal financial situation, but by

Wedding style in 1952. Note the interested bystanders.

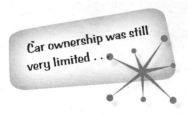

Car ownership was still very limited . .

no lesser person than the Chancellor of the Exchequer. Travellers abroad were not allowed to take more than £30 sterling out of the country. When purchasing traveller's cheques or foreign currency, a note of the amount was made in your passport; once that had gone there was no going to the bank or using a credit card (they were not in everyday use anyway) to draw more, so one had to learn to be economical.

Package holidays apart, the latter years of the 1950s also brought to the fore the use of cars. Car ownership was still very limited but petrol was now freely available, so it was often possible for a young couple either to hire or be loaned the use of a car. For these lucky ones, they still tended to follow the trend of making for the seaside for their honeymoon, though occasionally the local press, when giving a detailed report of a wedding, would add those magical, mysterious words, 'the honeymoon is to be spent touring', which certainly didn't imply an organised trip by coach, but rather a two-seater sports car and Scotland or the Lake District. One couple described driving to Italy to stay in the villa of an uncle, while another honeymooned in that most romantic of cities, Paris. Those who had married between 1950 and

1955 tended to have only a week away. The most likely destination was the seaside, and since money was a major concern this was often in a resort not that far away from home. A great advantage of living in the British Isles is that the coast is so accessible. Those brides who did not wish to be disappointed in their holiday destination either made suggestions as to where they wanted to go or dropped very broad hints if the husband-to-be was making the arrangements – unlike the bride who was promised a great surprise, only to find herself whisked off to a nearby resort that she particularly disliked. That certainly did not make for the easiest of starts to married life.

Accommodation for the week at the seaside was most likely to be in a bed and breakfast, hotel or boarding house. These acquired a reputation of being run by fearsome landladies who ruled the place with the proverbial rod. They were not the best of places for a young couple to stay as, having eaten breakfast, they were expected to vacate the premises and not return until the evening. And should they wish to return after 10.30 p.m. following a visit to the theatre or cinema, they had to inform the landlady and ask for a key. Although there would have been a washbasin in the bedroom, there was, of course, no such thing as an en suite bathroom; the one down the hall was shared with the other guests. There was no such thing either as a shower, and in some places you had to pay extra to have a bath, possibly having to place a 1s coin in the meter that provided the gas for the geyser that heated the water. All in all the accommodation could be pretty cheerless. But you were young and in love and provided the weather was reasonable, you really didn't mind.

If funds stretched that far then a hotel offered slightly more luxury – though you still didn't have your own bathroom! An alternative that provided accommodation and full board as well as lots of entertainment throughout the day was Butlins, or one of the smaller holiday camps dotted around the country, and many couples chose these. But a cheaper option to all these was to go to stay with relations, preferably fairly young ones that you liked, either in the country or, if you hankered for the bright lights, theatres, and museums

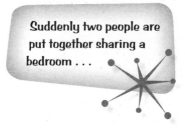

Suddenly two people are put together sharing a bedroom . . .

and art galleries, then what could be better than the aunts or cousins who lived close to London. Hop on a bus or take the Tube, an experience in itself for those from the provinces, and there was a whole world waiting to be discovered.

After all, discovery was what a honeymoon was all about in those far-off days. This was the first opportunity the majority had to find out much about the other that had been hidden – not least what lay beneath their clothing. It is not a cliché to say that most girls had never seen a man naked. Suddenly two people are put together sharing a bedroom and having to decide who sleeps on which side of the bed. This was the time when illusions could be shattered: that beautiful curly hair was achieved with the use of metal curlers, his toenails needed cutting and his feet could smell. But for that one week, it didn't really matter, there was a whole lifetime ahead of them to sort

out or get used to such things. Come the end of the week, they would be making a home together. Listening to ladies talking about their early lives and then reading through the answers from others to my questions, it became apparent that despite the contributors to this book being dispersed throughout the country there was a strong similarity in the way they lived, as if there was a pattern that had to be adhered to.

3

A Home of Their Own

Except that it wasn't! At the end of the war in 1945, Britain was faced with an acute housing shortage in those large towns and cities that had suffered severe bomb damage. Often whole streets had been totally wiped out, while others that had been left were declared unsafe as a result of bomb blast. Attempts were made to repair as many of these as possible but there was still a big gap between the number of houses available and the numbers of those who needed them. The obvious solution was to build more, but that was not as easy as it sounds as building materials, particularly timber, were still in very short supply, so all new building was subject to various sorts of regulations and builders required licences to carry out operations. Quite apart from replacing the original housing stock, the increased demand for homes had been exacerbated by the demobilisation of the armed forces and an upsurge in marriages. Then there were the couples who had married during the war where the wife had either remained at home with her parents or had been in lodgings close to where her husband was serving. They now joined the queue of young couples who were searching for somewhere to call home.

Renting your home had been traditional in this country for endless generations. Only the very wealthy few actually owned property and, certainly since the early nineteenth century, it had been commonplace for both landowners and industrialists to provide their workers with housing for which a weekly rent was paid. Even members of the professional classes rented from a landlord. The more affluent tradesmen looking for somewhere to invest their money might buy a few houses or even a whole street of sitting tenants. So the idea of buying a house was not necessarily the average couple's first thought in 1950. Since

private builders were restricted as to the number of houses they could build for sale, which might in turn be rented out, it fell to the local authorities to provide homes for their area. In some parts of the country council houses had been depleted too by the bombing, so there was already a waiting list for replacements. Until a proper building programme could get under way and produce the required numbers, temporary measures were put into place. These included the revolutionary idea of erecting factory-made prefabricated bungalows.

Between 1945 and 1949, including that dreadfully bitter winter of 1947, over 150,000 of these temporary homes sprang up throughout the country, forming new estates. From the outside their lack of traditional brick and slate may have seemed odd but inside they were a revelation! There was a fair-sized living room that had a traditional coal fire with a modern back boiler that not only provided hot water on tap but also wafted warm air into the two bedrooms. There was also a modern bathroom with a heated towel rail. This was everything for which a young family yearned. But it was the kitchen that made most people truly envious. Small and compact, it was modern;

Woman using an oven to cook a chicken in the 1950s. *Mary Evans Picture Library/Interfoto*

everything, including the oven, was built in, but it also had something that was unheard of in the majority of houses at that time – a refrigerator. It was just like a scaled-down version of those kitchens one had seen in American films. With a small garden at the front and a larger one at the back, those tenants who were offered a prefab were considered to be living in the lap of luxury. These buildings were intended to have a limited life; twenty-five years was discussed. However, the photograph shown in the plate section, of part of a road on a large estate started in 1947, was taken in 2011! During their sixty-something years of service the houses have, of course, been renovated and updated but few of their present occupants wish to move.

Somewhat less successful were the 'Airey' houses, again factory made from reinforced concrete columns and slabs, topped with a flat roof. They had the traditional interior layout of a three-bedroom house but, externally, were not only somewhat austere to look at, but over the years developed structural problems. However, they served their purpose for a time, giving the local authorities a breathing space as they set about acquiring more land, often agricultural on the edges of town, in order to start a

proper building programme – once restrictions were lifted and supplies became available – of modern, well-designed homes for the post-war generation. In planning these estates, the architects, having looked at the narrow streets of small terraced houses of the past, took the opportunity presented to them of providing plenty of open spaces, using not only front gardens but also wide expanses of grass, often planted with trees, between the pavement and the road. Unfortunately, when the designers drew up their plans for the future, none of them foresaw the expansion of the car industry and so, although they also provided sizeable back gardens, they failed to leave sufficient space between each pair of semi-detached houses for either a parking space or a future garage. Thus it is that sixty years on, in many estates the once beautiful greenswards beyond the pavement are little more than elongated car parks.

To help overcome the housing shortage, those who had a home were encouraged to share theirs with others. Families who, during the war, had had either evacuees or soldiers billeted on them and had finally got their house back to themselves now found it was happening all over again, the only difference being that at least they were allowed to choose with whom they would share. Very few of the brides who married in the first few years of the 1950s went straight into a house of their own. Often a girl coming back from her honeymoon found herself returning to her old bedroom. The only difference was that now she had to share that room with her new husband. If the family home was large enough or there were no other children occupying a bedroom, then it might be possible for her parents to let the couple have the use of another room as a sitting room.

Many couples spent up to two years living with their family or in lodgings, often having their first baby in these cramped conditions. Those who had their names on their Local Authority Council housing list found that it was not simply a question of moving automatically up the list as the one at the top was housed. Each couple was assessed on a points system. Priority was given to those in essential services – doctors, nurses, midwives, firemen and policemen too if the local police force had insufficient housing stock of its own. Then came the families in greatest need. Some authorities insisted that to get a step towards the top of the list a couple had to have two children, an incentive that further increased the already rapidly rising birth rate.

It was a red-letter day when a couple were finally informed they had been allocated a house. However, in those parts of the country where the need was greatest, there could be a small snag – they were still expected to share it, this time with another young couple!

Many couples spent up to two years living with their family or in lodgings . . .

Young people starting to furnish a home today are governed by how much they can afford, either in actual cash or on their credit cards. In the early 1950s, apart from money, the major consideration was the dreaded 'dockets' or units. Like everything else during and immediately after the war, new furniture was rationed. Because of the shortage of imported wood, selected furniture manufacturers throughout the country had been required to produce goods made from homegrown supplies. This was known as utility furniture, and it carried the insignia of two capital Cs and a 41: CC41. Units to be used when buying furniture were initially limited to those who had lost their homes through the bombing or were recently married and were setting up home for the first time. If the marriage was called off before the actual ceremony took place then the units had to be handed back. The maximum allocation was sixty units with another ten for each child. A large wooden item such as a wardrobe was twelve units, a 4ft bedstead five, a dining table six, a complete kitchen cabinet eight – if you were running short then you might have the bottom cabinet for five and dispense with the top that required

Like everything else, new furniture was rationed . . .

three more. The government leaflet containing these figures has in bold type: 'No allowance can be made for lodgers or visitors.' Bearing in mind that furniture included such things as cots, high chairs and playpens, all requiring precious 'dockets', it is not surprising that there was a brisk trade in second-hand furniture. Recycling was at its peak as young couples happily accepted the unfashionable but no longer wanted items of friends and family or trawled through the contents of second-hand shops to find pieces that they could use. A coat of paint here, a good polish there and many redundant chests of drawers, washstands and old-fashioned wardrobes were given a new lease of life. If the wardrobe happened to be the sort where the clothes cupboard usually sat atop a long deep drawer, then the two could be parted and, if necessary, the drawer might find an entirely new use as a baby's first cradle.

However, by the time we get to the second half of the decade, restrictions were lifted, the furniture industry was in full swing and, moreover, private builders were building houses for sale. These too tended to be large estates of either small bungalows or semi-detached houses. Again, many were built without garages or the space for one, but

A coat of paint here, a good polish there . . .

the back garden would allow room for a shed to house the
family's bicycles, garden tools and possibly also the wringer
that came out on washday.

Most couples furnished their homes in the traditional
way set by their parents. At that time many beds still
consisted of a heavy iron frame with wooden head and
foot boards supporting a base made of coiled springs or
tightly woven mesh. On this was laid the mattress. The
thick feather mattress had mostly fallen into disuse except
for children and the elderly, most people having what
were known as flock mattresses. The outer covering of
strong cotton fabric, often printed in blue or red stripes,
was stuffed with waste wool and other materials. To ensure
overall evenness the flock was secured firmly in place at
regular intervals with circular discs of tufted thread which
went right through the mattress. The drawback to these
mattresses was that after years of wear the flock matted
into uncomfortable lumps and the tufted discs either came
out or else caused discomfort. The early forms of interior

A 1950s housewife in her modern kitchen. *Courtesy of Hearst Magazines*

sprung mattresses also had their drawbacks when, for some reason, one of the metal springs unravelled and poked through the mattress, perhaps giving the sleeper a nasty scratch. The firm of Slumberland, which had developed their interior sprung mattress in the 1930s, had their production severely curtailed by the war, but by the early 1960s they were leading the way to a revolution in the bed industry. In much the same way, there has been a major change in what goes on a bed.

In the 1950s most people covered the mattress with either a flannelette sheet or an old blanket. Sheets and pillowcases were invariably made of cotton and their quality, which depended on whether the cotton had come from Egypt or India, varied from very fine through to the very strong twill which took some getting used to, especially if an economical housewife had turned the sheet 'sides to middle' which, while moving the worn part to the edge of the sheet, left the joining seam right where one usually slept. Next came the woollen blankets which, more than likely, had been made in Whitney. These again were pretty universal: unbleached with possibly a couple of dyed blue or green stripes at each end. One blanket was usual for summer use, two in winter. When it came to tucking in the bottom corners of both sheets and blankets, the method used in hospital was recommended. With the edges of the top sheet folded over the blankets, the whole effect was one of precise neatness. Next came the eiderdown. This, as its name suggests, should have been made of down but, unless one had paid a lot for it, it was more likely to have been filled with the feathers of a chicken than those of the eider duck. Eiderdowns could be covered with prettily patterned cotton fabric or, more often than not, had the upper side in

a silk or satin material in a good, strong, plain colour, rose pink and gold being very popular. The problem with these was that they were not washable and had to be dry-cleaned. In the 1950s the bedding department of many large stores did a steady trade in the refurbishment of old eiderdowns. Finally, a bedspread or quilt, a single sheet of material that matched the eiderdown, may have covered the made bed. At night the quilt was removed and every morning on rising the bedclothes were folded back over the foot of the bed to allow it to be aired before being remade after one had breakfasted. It was a slatternly housewife indeed who left her bed unmade throughout the day.

In passing we should mention that, like so much else, bed sizes have changed. The most common size for a double bed was a width of 4ft. The more affluent had the larger 4ft 6in. Children's beds were likely to be either 2ft 6in or 3ft; the latter would comfortably accommodate two children.

As for the rest of the bedroom, a double wardrobe was standard, with, if one could afford it, an additional, smaller, gentleman's wardrobe. Gone, however, was the washstand.

With a bathroom in the house there was no longer any need for the china basin and water jug which stood on the marble top, anymore than one would dream of storing the matching chamber pot in the cupboard beneath. All these 'old-fashioned' articles were dispensed with; sold for next to nothing to second-hand dealers who sold them on to eager American tourists! The discarded washstands themselves were stripped of their marble tops and re-covered with a wooden top to re-emerge as small sideboards. There would, however, be a dressing table with either a single or triple mirror and possibly a chest of drawers or tallboy – an interesting piece which had two or perhaps three drawers at the bottom with a two-door cabinet above. These were to prove very chic and useful a few years later for housing a television set, or, in some cases, as a cocktail cabinet – but we're straying now into the 1960s. Flooring throughout the house was likely to be a form of linoleum, which in the bedroom was covered with a rug on either side of the bed.

Downstairs, the front room would eventually hold the three-piece suite of sofa and two armchairs, with other luxury items following when the couple could afford them. For many, the dining room was still considered the family living room, with the matching dining set of sideboard,

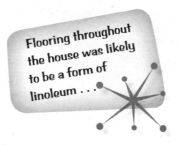

Flooring throughout the house was likely to be a form of linoleum . . .

table and four chairs. Two fireside armchairs, straight backed and with wooden arms, were placed where their name implied they should be. In the recesses beside the fireplace might stand the radiogram or a small table with the wireless on top and perhaps a standard lamp. On the other side might be a tea trolley, on the shelves of which would be kept magazines, and the housewife's sewing basket or knitting bag. Shelves at head height might also be fitted into the alcoves to serve as a bookcase or to display ornaments. The top of the sideboard almost always had the wedding-present clock as well as any pieces of wedding-present silver.

Perhaps the biggest change from the 1950s has occurred in the design of the kitchen. From the Industrial Revolution to the 1930s, the kitchen had been the smallest room in the house, often seeming to be an afterthought to the main building. Even in larger Victorian and Edwardian houses, there was a small scullery where food was prepared and the washing up done, while the actual cooking was done on a coal-fired range in what later became known as the breakfast room. In the two-up, two-down house, the tiny kitchen/scullery often contained a built-in stone copper

Perhaps the biggest change was in the design of the kitchen . . .

in one corner in which water was heated on washday and to fill the tin bath on bath night – usually Saturday – and even, recalling Dickens's *Christmas Carol*, to boil puddings. Cooking was done on the fire in the living room, and was often limited to what could be cooked in a saucepan or frying pan, though some fire grates incorporated a small oven to one side of the fire.

In the scullery or back kitchen, unless one was very fortunate to possess what was known as a butler's deep white sink, the standard was a very shallow one made of 'dried-on mustard' yellow stoneware, the outside of which carried a pattern of indentations in which grime could collect. In many families all forms of washing revolved around this sink, from personal ablutions and the weekly laundry to washing up after each meal. For each of these operations a bowl was placed inside the sink; originally it would have been an enamel one but by the 1950s was more likely to be made of plastic. In the days before liquid detergents were generally available, the housewife would have added a handful of household washing soda to the water before washing the dishes. For those who did not have hot water on tap, it was important to follow the old rules of washing up, that is, start with the cleanest objects

. . . it was usual to rinse glassware in clean cold water before drying and polishing.

like glassware and work through to the dirtiest and greasiest dishes and pans. While all were left to drain on the wooden draining board (although sometimes plates would be drained in a rack above the sink), it was usual to rinse glassware in clean cold water before drying and polishing. The inside of the standard yellow sink was very difficult to clean, especially when tea-stained. Invariably, in one corner stood a triangular-shaped strainer into which was tipped, at least three times a day, the leaves from the teapot. Added to throughout the day were vegetable peelings, especially potatoes, and occasional eggshells. At the end of the day the contents of the strainer were put on the living room fire to damp it down and keep it smouldering overnight, so that it could be brought to life again in the morning to boil a kettle for the breakfast cup of tea.

Before I am accused of wandering away from the 1950s, I need to assure the reader that there were many homes throughout the country, particularly in rural areas, where these conditions existed; for many a young housewife of the 1950s this was normal, everyday living. Similarly, there were still houses in towns without electricity where the occupants relied on gas for lighting as well as cooking. Those rural areas that were without either utility had to rely on paraffin oil lamps for lighting and either coal-fired stoves or cookers that ran on bottled gas. Although there were very few town dwellings that were not connected to water mains and sewerage – though not necessarily with a lavatory indoors – the same cannot be said for all country dwellings; many of those living in the country still had to draw their water from a well or a pump and use either an earth or chemical closet housed in a shed in the garden.

The new builds of the post-war period were of a different shape to houses of the Victorian and Edwardian eras. Instead of the thin rectangle with a half-rectangle extension we now had the totally rectangular house. A pretty standard design had the kitchen and the dining room stretching right across the back of the house with, in many cases, the kitchen larger than the dining room, which in turn was often separated from the sitting room by double glass doors rather than a wall. It would not be long before the separate dining room would give way to the L-shaped living room.

These new, larger kitchens still followed the traditional pattern of placing the sink under the window. At last deep white sinks replaced the horrible yellow ones, and in the early part of the 1950s wooden draining boards would be either side of the sink, each supported on a metal framework. Connections were provided for either gas or electric ovens which, once manufacturers were free to produce new designs, were a world away from the heavy black gas stoves or the blue mottled electric ovens of the past, both of which took up room. At this stage, a walk-in larder, or at least a large cupboard would have been part of the design so there was storage space. That, with a table and a couple of kitchen chairs, was that as far as the kitchen was concerned. No built-in units yet. A curtain in front of the sink framework hid buckets and cleaning materials, saucepans and possibly the Burco boiler – of which more later. But the item that most couples purchased, as soon as they could afford it, was the kitchen cabinet. Painted green, this had two round or oval frosted glass panels in the top cupboard in which one stored dry goods ready to use when cooking. Then came the enamel-covered fold-down flap on which you prepared your pastry and so on. Previously all baking had been carried out on the kitchen table – a plain wooden surface that could be scrubbed after use. But the modern kitchen cabinet provided the equivalent of the 1950s work surface, though, of course, that terminology had yet to be coined for the kitchen. One of the exciting things about this cabinet was the incorporated flour holder which, theoretically, should have emptied out its contents on to the enamel board. Another feature was the small, circular, mesh-covered disc in the doors, which allowed fresh air to circulate within the cupboard. The base of the cabinet held two further storage cupboards.

The idea that one day they would be able to afford a refrigerator hardly ever crossed the mind of the average housewife at the beginning of the 1950s. She had, of course, seen that they appeared to be standard in the American homes depicted on the cinema screen but she knew that anything similar was far too big for a kitchen like hers. However, by the end of the decade, small fridges

. . . by the end of the decade, small fridges were available.

were available. But until that day came, our housewives continued to do as their mothers had done, buying fresh food daily and using a 'meat safe', preferably in a cold larder, to keep meat fresh and away from flies.

The espresso coffee bars that arrived in major cities in the mid-1950s introduced the public to the use of both heatproof glass cups and saucers as well as the very colourful sheets of Formica that covered tabletops and counters. Manufacturers began producing more and more small kitchen tables covered with bright blue or yellow Formica and it wasn't long before the material was in great demand for what became the beginning of the fitted kitchen. Once the white sink had been replaced by the moulded enamel sink and draining board that was fitted into a wooden unit that housed under-sink cupboards, it was not long before shops were selling whitewood wall and floor cupboards for the homemaker to install and paint to his or her own taste. By the very end of the 1950s, house builders were beginning to realise that the fitted kitchen was what the public wanted.

In the meantime, it was a question of DIY for those who wanted to get ahead of fashion. In this, magazines played a very large part. One of the criticisms often levelled at life in the 1950s was that the stereotypes of male and female roles were reinforced, in particular in children's books where little girls, always depicted wearing a frilly apron, helped Mummy to do household chores while little boys helped Daddy in the garden or tool shed, perhaps mending a puncture to a bicycle. However, a well-known women's magazine shows a different picture. In a series of articles subtitled 'Save money and enjoy yourself', it promised that the series would help 'to make your kitchen your pride and joy'. One article was dedicated to flooring the kitchen. In the days before lino tiles were available, it was suggested that you could make your own quite cheaply. Having first measured the area of your floor ('turning it into square feet by multiplying the width by the length'), you then needed to buy about four offcuts of lino in different colours. Black, green, red and white were suggested. These were then cut into different sized squares and a patchwork design created. Clear, full details for the whole operation were given, accompanied by photographs of the various stages. What is interesting about these illustrations is that it was a collaborative effort; the young couple were to share the work between them and there was not a frilly apron in sight, the young woman being sensibly dressed in slacks and a sweater.

Having achieved a new floor, the following week's lesson was how to make a useful double cupboard to stand next to the cooker, which would also utilise those awkward few inches left in the corner by including a rounded projection of two open shelves. The whole unit was then topped by a continuous sheet of Formica. It may have taken them

Young Mr and Mrs 1950s wanted modern cutlery to suit their modern dining table.

longer than having units or a new kitchen floor fitted by a professional, but it would most certainly have cost them much less. Young Mr and Mrs 1950s wanted modern cutlery to suit their modern dining table. In this they were not disappointed. Manufacturers produced stainless steel as well as EPNS tableware in slim, elegant styles, light in weight and often much smaller in comparison to that of the previous generation. Out went the heavy, long-bladed knives with square bone handles and large forks. The steel knives that needed careful cleaning and sharpening (often done on the smooth stone step at the back door) were banished forever while the ancient hornhandled carving set came out only at Christmas: one of the eversharp Prestige kitchen knives being much more useful.

Stainless steel came in a variety of grades and consequently the cutlery varied from very cheap to very expensive; the former was thin and a bit tinny, whereas the most expensive could at a glance be taken for silver. If, however, the 1950s housewife yearned for silver rather than stainless steel, then she was helped in achieving her desire by probably one of the best advertising gimmicks of all time. In the middle of the 1950s Kelloggs launched their Insignia Plate cutlery offer. On each of their cereal packets was printed a token of different value according to the size of the packet. What started with an offer for six EPNS teaspoons for just a small payment plus a certain number of tokens, developed in time into the full range of cutlery. At a price one could afford and over a long period of time it was possible to have a complete table setting for six, including fish knives and forks, and, unlike most canteens of expensive cutlery that contained only two tablespoons, one could purchase six, if one wished. The elegant, somewhat classical, design was pleasing to the eye and each piece carried a twenty-five-year guarantee. As one who made use of this offer from Kelloggs, I can testify that most of it was in constant use for much longer than twenty-five years.

The other large item often given as a wedding present was the dinner service. Mothers-in-law often saw it as their prerogative to purchase the 'best' china for the newlyweds. Those who could afford it felt that there should be a

The coffee pot bearing the large sunflower was very popular . . .

matching dinner, tea and coffee set. Inevitably they would lean towards the makers and designs that had been popular in their own youth, or perhaps what they had hoped for and never had. The range of interesting shapes and use of unusual colours for crockery in some ways harked back to the designs of the 1920s and '30s, but to a generation which had grown up with a jumble of plates and so on left over from that time, mixed with even earlier ones either handed down or bought second hand and supplemented by the very plain utilitarian replacements available in wartime, these new pieces brought the promise of better times ahead. Midwinter probably produced most of the tableware bought in the 1950s, some of it being within an affordable price range. The coffee pot bearing the large sunflower was very popular, as was its design that moved right away from the traditional-shaped pot with the long curved spout. Other potteries like Poole and Denby produced larger cups and chunkier plates in unusual colours, sometimes combining two bold colours in a cup, the paler of the two on the inside. The sets produced by both these firms were comparatively expensive but it was possible to buy each piece individually. There was, it seems, a desire to return to more natural materials in some cases, one manufacturer opting for very heavy earthenware with the rim of each plate revealing the basic terracotta clay while the main piece was fired with a strong blue glaze with white spots. This surely was intended for everyday use; perhaps it was considered more masculine, but it was unlikely to impress your more aspiring friends.

From the modern pottery and dinky demi-tasse to the ultramodern plastic, which made it possible to equip your home with everything from a cup and saucer right through the range of tableware down to the matching eggcups, cruet set and jam pot. In bright colours and interesting shapes, plastic provided the housewife with the opportunity to choose between the rigid Melamine and the much lighter and less expensive plastic. The products that traded under the name of Melamine, Melaware or Gaydon were reputed to be so tough as to be unbreakable. It was the teacups that led to the eventual relegation of plastic tableware to the picnic basket or camping gear. The inner lining of the plastic cup was white and after a time the tannin in tea stained it very badly. But for a while plastic ruled, so much

It wasn't long before the United States would influence the British housewife yet again . . .

so, in fact, that the firm Midwinter actually produced its own version. It wasn't long before the United States would influence the British housewife yet again, this time taking over the kitchen with the now well-known Tupperware. Whatever anyone may have thought to the contrary, plastic in its many guises was here to stay.

4

'Twas on a Monday Morning...

We know from our history lessons that personal hygiene in the distant past was such that those with money smothered themselves with perfumes to cover the odours of others while the poor rarely removed their meagre clothing or submitted themselves to soap (which was very expensive) and water. So the population as a whole must have been inured to the manifold smells amongst which they lived. Which raises the question one hardly dare ask, namely, did we all smell in the 1950s? Certainly few of us changed into clean clothes daily. The development of new materials which can stand up to constant washing, as well as those which are machine washable, along with major advances in these new washing machines, has changed our habits. In the days when everyone wore jumpers and pullovers knitted from pure wool, these were items which required very careful washing. If the water was too hot, there was a strong likelihood of shrinking the garment or of it becoming matted. Woollens required careful handwashing with soap flakes rather than the more abrasive powders used for dirtier items, and also needed extra care in the drying process. Water had to be gently squeezed out of them; they needed to be dried flat rather than hung on a line – which could so easily stretch them – and never, ever, put them close to the fire to dry. Small wonder then, that men's thick sweaters in particular did not get washed as frequently as they should have done in those pre-male-deodorant days!

For the majority of stay-at-home housewives in the early 1950s, Monday was still regarded as washday. This was because, with the progress of time, it had become customary for the family to have a bath on Friday or Saturday night (whether one needed it or not, as one young man expressed it) and put on clean clothes for the week ahead. Although baths were rarely taken more than once a week, even in households where there was a bathroom, it was expected that each member of the family would have 'a proper' wash each morning before going off to work or school. This particular ablution was known as a strip wash, though some junior members were likely to forget that they had ears or underarms. The clothes worn during the week were then consigned to the laundry basket ready for Monday's wash.

Beds were stripped of their sheets and pillowcases; in households where bedding was in short supply, only the bottom sheet was changed weekly, the one that had been on the top taking its place on the bottom and a clean one coming in as a top sheet. This helped to lessen wear and tear. It was considered necessary to wash sheets at a very high temperature and, if possible, most housewives preferred to boil them along with other white linens such

Those on a tighter budget had the option of the 'bag wash'

as tablecloths. Sheets then were made of much stronger and heavier cotton than nowadays and, consequently, double sheets in particular were difficult to deal with. Those who could afford it sent their sheets, pillowcases and table linen to a commercial laundry, which returned them beautifully starched and ironed. Those on a tighter budget had the option of the 'bag wash' – the forerunner of the coin-operated launderettes, which made their appearance in the early 1950s. These huge wonderful machines, which like so much else brought echoes of American life, were very popular, provided you remembered to sort your whites from your colours.

However, for the majority, Monday meant lighting a copper, plugging in the electric Burco boiler or filling the sink from the Ascot water heater ready for the washing, which took most of the day. Once the washing had been rinsed thoroughly – and the whites put through an extra rinse that contained Reckitts blue – then the whole lot had to be wrung out to get rid of as much excess water as possible. This process required a very strong wrist action, something that over the years many women developed, but

Progress in the Home

Hoover Limited take pride in the fact that their products are saving millions of housewives from hard, wearisome drudgery — not only in Britain but throughout the world. Wherever the name Hoover appears it is a guarantee of excellence.

THE WORLD-FAMOUS HOOVER CLEANER

The Hoover Cleaner, with its famous triple-action principle — " It beats . . . as it sweeps . . . as it cleans " — is undeniably the world's best cleaner — best in design, best in materials, best in quality of workmanship. There is a model suitable for every size and type of home.

THE MARVELLOUS HOOVER ELECTRIC WASHING MACHINE

The Hoover Electric Washing Machine has completely revolutionised the whole conception of washing-day in the home. It does the full weekly wash for a large family and yet is such a handy size—suitable for even the smallest kitchen.

VISIT THE HOOVER FACTORY

Visitors to the Festival of Britain are cordially invited to make a tour of the Hoover Factories at Perivale, Middlesex, or Merthyr Tydfil, South Wales, or Cambuslang, Scotland. Please write to, Hoover Limited, Perivale, or 'phone Perivale 3311 for more information.

HOOVER LIMITED

Factories at :

PERIVALE, MIDDLESEX · MERTHYR TYDFIL · HIGH WYCOMBE · CAMBUSLANG, SCOTLAND

Advertisement for Hoover appliances that appeared in the 1951 Festival of Britain Guide. *Courtesy of Hoover-Candy* for those that didn't then the wringer or mangle had to be used. A wringer, on the other hand, was a much smaller and more compact 'modern' piece of equipment. Some were small enough to be clamped on to the draining board of the kitchen sink, while those on a stand were more robust.

Each load of washing was then hung out to dry on a line that straddled either the backyard or garden. When the line was full, a clothes prop – a long piece of wood with a V cut into the top – was slipped into the middle of the line and then elevated so the clothes could happily flap in the wind to dry. That was the theory. In practice, particularly in winter, the clothes were often still wet, or at least damp, when they were brought in. Some kitchens had a wooden drying rack suspended from the ceiling that could be let down; the damp laundry was then placed on it and it was hauled up again, leaving the laundry to dry overnight. Most families also had a clothes horse – not the plastic-covered thin metal, concertinatype airer but a proper wooden bi-fold stand (very handy when inverted for making a tent), which could be placed in front of the fire. Monday evenings in winter had their own, very special, smell!

There was just one ritual left to complete washday and that was 'the folding of the sheets'. Every child in the past must have served an apprenticeship in the art of holding the corners of sheets and tablecloths, learning not to let go at the wrong moment, how to make the correct folds and when to pull slightly on one side or the other to get them level, until they were ready for the following day when the housewife would do the ironing.

By the 1950s it was only those who lived in rural areas without an electricity supply who were still reliant on the flat iron heated on the fire. The urban dweller would have had an electric iron very similar to those we use nowadays, except, of course, there would not have been any steam irons. Everyone knew that water and electricity was a very dangerous mixture. If one needed to achieve the steam effect while ironing, the trick was to cover the item with a dampened cloth and run the iron gently over it, but one had to be very careful not to get any actual water on the sole plate of the iron as this could result either in a blown fuse or, at worst, the destruction of the iron's element.

... the 1950s housewife dreamed of cutting down on the hard physical labour of washday ...

Having plugged in the iron, our housewife would, in the early part of the 1950s, have ironed on the kitchen or living room table. Some women had a board that they placed upon the table – the leaf of an extending table was often used – covered with an old blanket or some other means of padding and topped with a clean piece of sheeting kept specifically for that purpose. Those wives who had several shirts and blouses to iron may have invested in a small portable wooden block, shaped to take the shoulders and sleeves of such garments. Although shaped heavy wooden ironing boards were available it was a real boon when the modern lightweight metal ironing board was introduced towards the end of the decade.

Then once she had the ironing board it wasn't long before the 1950s housewife dreamed of cutting down on the hard physical labour of washday by owning a washing machine to do the work for her. Hoover had advertised their machine at the Festival of Britain but it was not until the second half of the 1950s that smaller versions of the American models were being produced in British factories. They were expensive but often the decision to buy one was justified by the arrival of a baby and all the extra washing that would entail.

The English Electric Company introduced their machine in 1955. It was what became known as a top-loader. It was square, often a creamy yellow, had a lid that lifted off – just as the old copper lid had – and contained nothing more than a central revolving paddle. It was filled by connecting a hose to either of the taps on the sink. The machine could heat the water to boiling but obviously if one started off with hot water, this cut down on the time needed to reach the required temperature. Most housewives started off with their boil wash and, as the water cooled, added the more delicate items. This model included a wringer that normally sat at the back of the tub but, when rinsing and wringing took place, could swing out over the sink. When the washing was completed, the hose was hooked over the edge of the sink and the water was pumped out. The next development was the twin tub. Again it was a top-loading machine but instead of being square it had become an oblong with part of the space occupied by the washing area with its paddle, while the slightly smaller portion was a drum, which supplanted the

... it would be at least another ten years or so before the fully automated front-loading machine was introduced ...

wringer and spun at high speed to remove the water from the laundry. It was a major step forward but it would be at least another ten years or so before the fully automated front-loading machine was introduced and, with it, the revolution in types of detergent.

5

In Her Shopping Basket She Has…

We have already established that the 1950s housewife usually shopped daily for the fresh ingredients of the main meal of the day. Unlike today's housewife she tended to visit a number of different shops and she bought in small quantities. Since most wives had a set amount of money available for housekeeping they learned to shop wisely in order to make sure that there was enough to last for the week. The prudent woman had probably adopted her mother's habit of keeping a weekly account book. In this she would list the basic items she needed: a ¼lb packet of tea (loose leaves not tea bags), ½lb of butter, the same of cheese, mainly Cheddar, and cooking fat (lard or Trex) – cooking oil was unheard of, while for most people olive oil was still something you obtained in small quantities from the chemist and used warmed to cure earache. Britons were, of course, still using imperial measures, so everything came in pounds and ounces. Eggs, flour, jam and marmalade, peanut butter, Marmite, Bovril or Betox, cocoa or Ovaltine, bacon (back for preference, streaky if you were hard up) – these were likely to feature regularly, if not weekly, on the list. It could be enlivened with occasional treats such as Libby's tinned fruit, peaches or fruit cocktail, evaporated milk and the inevitable Bird's custard powder.

Most of these could be obtained from one of the old established grocers in one's neighbourhood. Having placed her order, the 1950s customer could sit on the chair in front of the counter as the grocer or his assistant assembled each item in front of him, making conversation as he did so, perhaps discussing the merits of different brands of baked beans before ticking off each item in the order book and noting its price in the column down the side. This allowed the customer the chance to compare current prices with those of previous weeks and if the rise was too much she would know where to make cuts the following week. Her basket was then packed for her, the column of figures added up, and the pounds, shillings and pence in her purse passed either across the counter or taken to the small kiosk

in the corner where the matriarchal lady who dealt with matters financial reigned aloof from all.

Of course, not all shops were owned by independent traders. Every town possessed at least one branch of one of the nationwide chains such as The Maypole, The International, David Greig, Elmers, Kays, The Home and Colonial, Liptons and Sainsbury's. In time each of these developed multiple service counters where the customer moved from one to the other. Ask any woman who was either a child or a housewife in the 1950s for memories of shopping and without a doubt she will mention Sainsbury's. Their shops tended to be long and narrow from front to back with one long counter stretching down each side. Gleaming white-patterned tiles covered the walls and with the chequerboard tiled floor they created an aura of ultra cleanliness. All the assistants wore white overalls and caps on their heads. But it was the butter and cheese counters that evoked most memories. With hindsight this may have been a reaction to the after-effects of rationing but who could not fail to be impressed by those enormous mounds of golden butter that stood against the walls? And how we marvelled at the mastery of the assistant who, with two

large wooden paddles, could remove a small piece from the yellow mountain, pat it into a neat rectangle which, when placed on the scales, weighed exactly the 8oz that had been requested. To those who had grown up accustomed to taking their butter ration as it came it was sheer delight to be able to choose if one would have English butter or that from New Zealand or Denmark, salted or unsalted. Choice was governed by price or preference for taste.

Similarly there was now a choice of cheeses. Like the butter, whole wheels of cheese were on display and again one would admire the precision with which the assistant would cut your desired amount with a very fine wire ready for the scales. These scales themselves were worth looking at. Made of brass with a pan either side of a central beam, your butter or cheese was placed in one pan and the different weights, also made of brass, some of which resembled chess pieces, were placed in the other. From dairy products one would pass down the counter to where the large, red, somewhat frightening, slicing machine held pride of place. Here were to be found whole sides of bacon and hams, and again one could choose exactly how much of which one wanted. You watched almost breathlessly as the circular blade of the slicer passed through the bacon or ham joints cutting to the thickness for which you had asked. Your order was then carefully wrapped in greaseproof paper. And so you worked your way up and down the counters. As each item was purchased the customer was given a small ticket bearing the price of the item, and before she left the shop she would take these to settle her bill at the polished wood, glass-fronted cashier's desk that was situated at the far end of the shop.

The ordinary butcher's shop usually still had sawdust on the floor to make it easier to clear up anything that fell from

Your butcher could be your best friend . . .

joints being cut. As our housewife watched, the butcher chopped or sawed through bones before cutting off the joint she had requested with a lethally sharp knife. Your butcher could be your best friend for he not only knew how each joint should be cooked, but could also advise the novice cook on what would be right for her budget. He would cut the stewing beef or shin for a pie or casserole into cubes and add just the right amount of ox kidney if she was making a steak and kidney pudding, usually throwing in for nothing the lump of suet she would need to make the pudding crust.

Continuing with her shopping, our housewife might next visit a bakery and confectioner's shop for a fresh crusty loaf of bread and perhaps, if mother-in-law was coming to tea on Sunday, a cake. Faced with the array of chocolate eclairs, iced buns, Eccles cakes and cream doughnuts, all freshly made on the premises, our housewife might decide to play it safe and select instead a Fuller's iced Madeira cake. This was always very popular, as were a Battenberg or a Lyons chocolate Swiss roll. If the bakery was part of one of the chains, such as the ABC which stood for the Aerated Bread Company, then the shop might have had a small café in the back where one could, if one so wished,

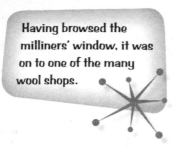

Having browsed the milliners' window, it was on to one of the many wool shops.

sit down and have a cup of tea before continuing with the shopping.

Our housewife did not spend all her time on food shopping. If she needed a new hat, for example, she again had choice from among the specialist milliners, of which there were usually several in town. It is possible that the very term 'millinery' has fallen into disuse, rather as the wearing of hats has. But in the 1950s there were still skilful ladies who could make a hat for you to wear for a special occasion, as well as keeping a good stock of ready-made ones, copies of which they could guarantee would not be found on the counters of Marks & Spencer or British Home Stores. Having browsed the milliners' windows, it was on to one of the many wool shops. The housewife might have been there to collect the last few ounces of wool for the cardigan she was making for her husband.

Apart from the plethora of wool shops, most towns also supported sewing-related shops. In the shops Leisure Hours, Busy Fingers and Spare Moments the enthusiast could buy linen to embroider or a design-ready printed tray cloth or tablecloth that came with the directions as to which of the wide range of Clark's Anchor stranded silks

should be used to complete it. Here too were to be found not only the different types of canvas for tapestry work and the accompanying wools but also frames for holding the work in progress. One never seemed to be hurried in these establishments as like-minded ladies congregated to discuss the relative merits of different items. Now that she has done all her shopping and doesn't need to hurry home because her husband will not yet have returned from either

... elegant tea rooms with waitresses in black dresses and frilly white aprons ...

playing in a match or watching the local football team, she may meet a friend at one of the many tea rooms or cafés in town. There were those behind specialist coffee shops like the Kardomah where the smell of coffee roasting in a machine in the window wafted out into the street, enticing

A woman shopping in the frozen food aisle of a supermarket.
Mary Evans/Classic Stock/H. Armstrong Roberts

China rather than the everyday Indian to which she was accustomed, and she would eat her chosen cake or pastry with a pastry fork, something she rarely, if ever, used at home. Alas, such elegance was not to last. Gradually the tea rooms would become either self-service snack bars or, towards the end of the decade, coffee bars. No longer would our 1950s housewife be able to relax over her tea and scones while a lady pianist accompanied a violinist in a selection of gentle popular classics to soothe away the cares of the day.

6

Leisure Time

The research for this book suggests that young married couples did not go out very much in the 1950s. Mr and Mrs Average may have gone to the cinema once a week or to a dance on Saturday night but most did not have the money to spend on entertainment, so they spent their evenings at home. Most people lived close enough to their workplace to be home by six o'clock, so once they had eaten their evening meal and washed up, they had at least three hours at their leisure before bedtime. This was the era before television had taken control of most people's evening activities. It is generally recognised that it was the televising of the Coronation on 2 June 1953 that persuaded families, in particular, to undertake the expense of installing a television set. Quite apart from the high price of the set itself, there was the additional quite heavy cost of installing an aerial on the roof, plus the annual licence fee. Although it was possible to hire a set at a reasonable monthly payment or to buy it on 'the never-never', as hire-purchase agreements were known, throughout the country as a whole sets were few and far between. Often housed inside a magnificent mahogany cabinet with doors, which closed when it was not in use, was a tiny screen, just 9in wide, smaller than the modern computer notebook. This meant that viewers had to sit quite close to it in order to get a clear picture. And very lucky you were if the picture was clear. Reception depended on how close one was to the local station that was relaying the signal. In those early days, only the BBC had a licence to show television programmes and even when ITV came into operation, reception in many parts of the country remained weak – a bit like broadband today!

Many people's first viewing was of a picture seen through an ultra-thick magnifying glass that overlaid the screen. These additional aids were in great demand for the Coronation, when proud television owners invited friends and members of their extended families to join them for the occasion. Often there was only one set in a whole street – you knew where it was, of course, by the aerial on the roof – and you jostled for an invitation. It seems incredible now that the daily transmission time was so short; that Sunday night programmes didn't start until after the time when evening church services ended and that each evening's programme concluded before midnight with the playing of the National Anthem. As the company assembled, curtains were drawn to shut out the daylight, the overhead electric light was extinguished, and a small table lamp, placed either on or near the set, for the sake of one's eyes, gave the only illumination. Apart from special events, television viewing at this stage was for the affluent, the elderly or families; young couples preferred to occupy their time listening to the radio, which provided plenty of diverse entertainment from variety shows, comedy programmes or plays, both

A 1950s couple watching television. Mary Evans/Classic Stock/H. Armstrong Roberts

original new drama or the dramatisation in serial form of classic books like *The Forsyte Saga* – which later became one of the first major Sunday night television dramas. There was plenty of opportunity too to listen to music on the radio, both on the Light Programme and on the commercial station, Radio Luxembourg, which introduced us to advertising from an early age by inducing children to become Ovalteenies. There were so many favourite radio programmes from the 1950s that, as with the novels, theatre plays and films, they will be included in appendices at the end of this book.

A young couple might not be able to afford a television set but many would save up to buy either a radiogram or a portable record player so that they could listen to their favourite music. The radiogram, as its name implies, incorporated both radio and gramophone into one impressive piece of living room furniture. This was a variation of what had existed in most homes in the 1940s:

a wind-up gramophone in a simple cabinet which housed the speakers as well as space to store the records and, on top of which, stood the imposing 'wireless'. Imposing not only because of its size but because during those war years it had been the means of keeping the nation informed of the progress of the war. But the 1950s saw many of these old-fashioned pieces discarded. The wireless, especially one that was powered by a cumbersome accumulator that had to be taken to a shop to be 'topped up', was consigned to the rag-and-bone man who still toured the streets – if not with a horse and cart like *Steptoe and Son*, then in a lorry – while the old gramophone cabinet was likely to be recycled by an ardent DIY member of the family into a cocktail cabinet. Quite how many families actually drank cocktails is another 1950s mystery but the gramophone cabinet was not alone in suffering a makeover; in time the radiogram went the same way, as did many pianos, their interiors ripped out to be replaced with fitted lights which reflected against chromium tiles.

In retrospect, although the 1950s saw great leaps forward in so many areas, it was also a period when, in

. . . if you heated these pre-vinyl records it was possible to mould them into interesting shapes . . .

the urge to be 'modern', what can only be described as acts of vandalism took place. This is not the place to draw attention to the wholesale clearing of ancient buildings in some towns and their replacement with monstrous grey cement-clad blocks of flats; I'm thinking more of artistic crazes such as that which led to the destruction of precious old 78rpm records. Someone discovered that if you heated these pre-vinyl records it was possible to mould them into interesting shapes which could be used as ornamental fruit bowls and the like. Thousands must have been sacrificed as this fad hit the country.

Fortunately, our young married wife was unlikely to have succumbed to such desecration in her efforts to beautify her home. She had much more practical projects in hand so while she and her husband listened in the evening to the radio or to records, she was busy making things. Most new housewives in the 1950s had grown up in the wartime atmosphere of 'make do and mend'. They had watched their mothers and grandmothers knitting and sewing and had learned to do likewise. What was not learned at home might be taught in school where, even from an early age, they had been encouraged to make the ubiquitous Christmas paper chains using strips of coloured paper stuck at the ends with flour and water paste. Using that same paste mixture, once newspaper or scrap paper was available, children would be taught how to make papier mâché bowls and dishes, which were then decorated using the little blocks of paint in their paintbox. While still children, girls were encouraged to make presents for members of the family for Christmas and birthdays; knitted kettle holders, pincushions and needle cases, covered coat hangers, embroidered hankies, all these were appreciated by the recipients as much, if not more, than any expensive gift today that has the child's name on it yet is known to have been paid for by the parent.

So our housewife was no novice when it came to making a house into a home. To start with there were curtains to be made for each room in the house, then there were cushion covers and padded seat covers for dining chairs, tablecloths and dressing table sets … the list went on. All these items were, of course, now available in the shops but making them yourself saved money. A popular pastime of the period, which was often a joint project, was

rug making. There were two sorts of rug one could make. One had long been a standby of those on limited incomes and was made from remnants of material or rags. In its very basic form one could use an old sack, opened up to form the backing, and then, having cut up as many discarded old clothes and other bits of fabric as one could find into strips, these were threaded, a piece at a time, through the holes in the sacking to form a tuft on the right side of what would eventually become the rug. It was a time-consuming but totally satisfying operation, allowing one endless opportunity for creativity in the design, and the end result was not only colourful and unique, but it was also extremely warm to the feet. At a time when bedroom floors, for example, were still covered with cold, shiny lino, a rag mat either side of the bed was undoubtedly better than nothing at all.

However, if you had sufficient funds and you desired to have a hearthrug fitted to grace your living room, then you could take the option of buying a 'Readicut' rug kit. This, as its name implies, had everything one required to produce a decorative rug: a new canvas stamped with the design and sufficient wool, separated into each colour and all cut into the correct length, to complete the design. Full instructions were included as was the latchet hook that was needed to pass the wool back and forth. These rugs, which came either as semi-circular or the standard oblong, were most attractive, and gave not only a luxurious feel to the room but brought the couple a tremendous feeling of satisfaction. In the same way, if they had furnished their home with second-hand furniture, they could take pride and pleasure in renovating or embellishing it. For a few pence and with a bit of ingenuity a couple of orange boxes nailed together and covered with a pretty piece of offcut material could become a useful additional storage cupboard in the bedroom or bathroom.

The housewife who enjoyed handicrafts was well served by helpful magazines, including the popular monthly *Stitchcraft*, which in July 1950 cost 9*d*. Still suffering from post-war paper restrictions, this edition ran to a mere twenty-two pages, which included amongst its items a pattern for crocheted summer gloves and an 'adorable little cap you can make in an evening' made from a piece of white felt with an intricate design worked in black thread. Unfortunately, the transfer for the design as well as the pattern for the four pieces which made up the cap had to be obtained from the magazine at a cost of 8*d* (post free). However, the enterprising housewife might be able to fabricate her own patterns. Among the patterns for jumpers, there was also an embroidered table place setting, described as a luncheon set, and a page of recipes of summer sweets – apple crumble, coffee cream and a fruit roll.

Even if she sent her sheets to the laundry, there were still her husband's shirts to be pressed.

When our housewife tired of using her sewing machine to make dresses or run up curtains for the whole house, or plying her knitting needles to make winter hats and scarves or socks for her husband, and when she'd run out of places to put crocheted doilies and place mats, if she was enterprising she could take up her tapestry needle instead and create a picture in wool to cover a chair seat or put into a fire screen to cover the empty grate in summer. Stitchcraft, like the women's magazines of the period, also prepared the young housewife for eventual motherhood, and so the wise young woman carefully stored away her back issues for future use.

However, we are not to suppose that our housewife spent every evening occupied with handicrafts. If she was still holding down a job, then she would devote at least one evening to catching up on the ironing. Even if she sent her sheets to the laundry, there were still her husband's shirts to be carefully pressed. Although in those days one didn't necessarily wear clean clothes every day, your husband's work might demand a clean white shirt daily and before the arrival of easycare cotton, that meant a lot of ironing –

and without the assistance of a steam iron. No wonder then that our housewife jumped at the chance to get outside and share the gardening with her husband, both of them gaining satisfaction from growing as many of their own vegetables as possible. If they were country dwellers, or had a suburban garden that was big enough, they could well have kept hens, giving them an egg supply and the occasional treat of a roast chicken when the hen had passed its laying days.

Many cafés and restaurants outside London kept shop hours and closed in the evening. Those that were open would have been considered beyond the price range of most people. It would be well into the 1960s before ordinary folk would consider entering the big hotel in the centre of town and sitting down to dine in the evening amongst those who were staying there. However, as a special treat they might have lunch in a café on a Saturday, or possibly an afternoon tea of scones and cake. If they were celebrating they might even manage a last order of sausage, beans and chips before going off to queue for the cinema on a Friday evening. If they hadn't managed to eat before the film started, then, if they were out in time, which might mean missing the last few minutes, they might catch the fish-and-chip shop before it too closed.

The traditional English public house was still very much part of the 1950s landscape. In many ways it was still considered 'man's territory', though concessions had been made in those establishments big enough to have separate bars to have one labelled as the 'lounge bar'. Here a couple could sit on comfortable chairs at a small table rather than standing at the bar amid all the masculine

> **Although a man might take his wife into the pub, women visiting on their own were not encouraged.**

talk. The 1950s wife would probably drink a Babycham, or a Britvic fruit juice, possibly a glass of Merrydown cider or, if she was very daring, a lemonade and beer shandy. It was likely too that both she and her husband smoked a cigarette while they were there and possible that they shared a packet of Smith's crisps. These were the forerunner of modern-day crisps, and were memorable because not only were they just simple plain potato but each packet contained a tiny screw of blue paper in which was the salt for you to sprinkle into the bag. The mind boggles now at the thought that in those bygone days there were workers whose job it was to place the required amount of salt on to that small square of paper and then to screw it up tight. Years later Smith's attempted to bring back the salt, packing it into machine-sealed sachets, but it was not the same as the original.

Although a man might take his wife into the pub, women visiting on their own were not encouraged. No doubt this unspoken embargo had its roots in the ladies of the night who once used the pubs to ply their trade.

The pub also gave the opportunity for games such as shoveha'penny, dominoes, darts and perhaps skittles in the adjoining skittle alley. There was no restriction on women playing either of the last two. Many young couples would entertain themselves in the evenings with a game of cards. Again, most of them had been brought up in the previous decade when whist was very popular, both in the home and as a social function as children; they would have been taught to play whist, as well as other suitable card games. Cards crossed not only the social divide but the generations too when extended family gatherings were held. Those aspiring to ascend the social ladder learned to play bridge and could then entertain like-minded couples to an evening devoted to the game. A couple on their own might pit their wits against each other with a game of cribbage, while for an evening of bluff and double bluff and keeping a poker face there was nothing to beat a game of canasta. This was also a good game to play with friends who had come to supper or perhaps just a drink.

The 1950s
produced some very
fine literature . . .

Pleasures were simple in those days. If our 1950s housewife was the outgoing artistic type with a good voice, she might join a choir, perhaps one belonging to her church, or the amateur operatic society or a group dedicated to performing the works of Gilbert and Sullivan. If not a singer but a musician, then it was obvious she would join with others to make music, whether it was playing chamber music or in a brass band. Belonging to an amateur dramatics group was also very popular throughout the 1950s, giving those who took part the opportunity to enjoy acting or help backstage with scenery-making or costume design. These groups also served a much wider social purpose by presenting audiences with the opportunity to see plays that might otherwise never be within their reach.

For the couple who were not so extrovert and who were quite happy to stay in, particularly on cold winter evenings, then reading was the answer. The 1950s produced some very fine literature, most of which was available to the general public at little or no cost at all. Most urban areas had not only a central public library, which seemed to house every book ever published, but a well-stocked reference library where it was possible to go and sit in silence to study those books which you could not actually borrow. Finally, and usually near the main entrance, was a reading room that housed large, sloping easel–type structures on which were displayed most of the daily newspapers. Here you could browse your way through the important political events of the day without the expense of buying a national newspaper or, if you were job hunting, then you could scour the situations vacant column of the local paper. The reading room was always well used. It was warm there in winter, often providing a haven for 'gentlemen of the road' who had nowhere else to go in bad weather. Retired gentlemen often passed the time there reading while they waited for their wives to finish the shopping. In large towns the local authorities also provided smaller branch libraries in areas of dense housing, so no one was ever far from the opportunity to borrow books for free.

There were two alternatives to the free public library: the local newsagent and Boots the Chemist. Neighbourhood newsagents often had space within their shop or possibly in a back room to house several shelves of books. As a customer of the newsagent who delivered your daily paper, you paid a small subscription to join his library, paying

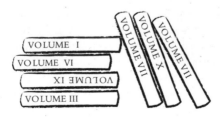

threepence or so to borrow a book for a set period of time. Like the public library, a minimal fine was imposed if the book was returned late. The novels available – romances, detective stories and thrillers – catered for popular tastes. A slightly upmarket version of the newsagent–library was provided by Boots. As early as 1898, the beneficent founder of the company had put into his first shop a 'booklover's library', thus spreading his desire to offer education to all. By the 1950s a certain social cachet had developed in holding a Boots library card and it continued to offer a wide selection of both fiction and non-fiction.

Those who loved books began to build their own libraries. These were not the matching leather-bound books that were placed on a bookshelf or in a glass-fronted cabinet to impress visitors, but the books they really wanted to read. These were now brought within their scope by the paperbacks produced by Penguin, who published not just novels but a whole range of literature from classical Greek authors in translation, right through to the poetry, plays and nonfiction of the twentieth century. Penguin and Dent's Everyman series between them opened the eyes of many to the great world that lies within a book.

In considering the leisure activities of the 1950s housewife, we must not forget sports. Many young women continued to play competitive tennis, netball and hockey while they could. Their husbands probably played football, rugby and cricket, in which case the wife was likely to be involved on the domestic side by providing refreshments, particularly for cricket teas. She would also find herself washing his games kit! A wife may have accompanied her man to watch the local professional football team and both may have been keen members of their local swimming club. Membership of a golf club was often an aspiration for many rising young businessmen, but it was an expensive sport in England, though not in Scotland. Younger women were not drawn so much to golf, possibly because many clubs were still very much a male preserve, but they might well have the strong arm and good eye necessary for membership of an archery club, which provided them with exercise in the open air. All in all there was plenty to keep the 1950s housewife and her husband busy and amused.

Finally we come to what was the one leisure activity which cut across all classes of society and was probably in its heyday in the 1950s – going to the cinema. Whether one lived in a town with three or four cinemas or in a rural area, which meant a journey by bus or a bike ride to the nearest town, most people visited the cinema fairly regularly. Admission was still quite reasonably priced; if you didn't mind getting a crick in the back of your neck the first few rows closest to the screen cost as little as 1*s*. The back row downstairs in some cinemas had double seats, and these were usually occupied by courting couples. In

those days the cinemas tended to open just after lunch, between one and two o'clock and although they gave the times that the films would be shown, the programmes ran continuously. It did not matter if you did not arrive in time for the start of the film, you took your seat anyway and waited until such time as the part you had missed came round again. Apart from the big American musicals such as *Annie Get Your Gun*, *Guys and Dolls* and *The Pajama Game*, most cinemas were still showing two films in each programme. With every 'big' picture there would be the 'B' film, perhaps a short black-and-white murder mystery with detectives in trilby hats and raincoats chasing villains in out-of-date cars that had a bell clanging on top. These films often had the audiences convulsing with laughter, although this was not the case when they were confronted with the realism of the police drama *The Blue Lamp*.

The films of the 1950s varied widely in their subject matter from those that retold the events of the Second World War, like *The Dambusters*, *The Colditz Story* and *Ice Cold in Alex*, to political comment in *I'm All Right Jack* and *Passport to Pimlico*, to sheer escapism in *High Society* and *Around the World in Eighty Days*. All these films would have been watched with pleasure and enjoyment despite

> . . . occasionally it was possible to see the hovering smoke caught up in its beam.

the fact that many of the audience would have viewed them through a haze of cigarette smoke. In those days an ashtray was placed between every other seat, fixed to the back of the seat in front. By the end of an evening most of these were overflowing. Films were projected from a box at the rear of the cinema and occasionally it was possible to see the hovering smoke caught up in its beam. The picture being shown came on several heavy reels of film and the projectionist had to ensure that he played each reel in the correct order, making sure that the next one was wound ready to go before the previous one ran out. Occasionally mishaps occurred; the wrong reel was put on or, worse, the machine broke down causing a hiatus. It seemed then as if this always happened at the most exciting part of the film. Nevertheless, having seen a tantalising trailer for the following week's programme, most people departed for home satisfied with a good evening's entertainment.

7

Putting on the Style

After all the years of austerity and restrictions, suddenly here were revolutionary new designs in women's clothes. The emphasis was on the word 'new' yet anyone who knew anything about the past realised that what Dior had done was to take his inspiration from the turn of the century. Instead of the knee-length skirts of the 1940s and the straight-cut suit jackets, hemlines were dropped almost to the ankle, waists were nipped in to resemble those highly corseted 18in ones of late Victorian times, and some designs even attempted a bustle effect. It was all quite mind-boggling – and of course – 'not for us'.

However, it was not long before the couture designs were adapted for the high street and the ankle-length hemline retreated up to the calf. The pencil skirt worn with a neat frilly blouse tucked in at the waist was very popular for young business women while the older woman opted for the complete ensemble of the fitted jacket, which emphasised the waist. The drop in skirt length had an unexpected impact on, of all things, the gymslip worn by schoolgirls. This universal garment, consisting of three box pleats front and back, fastened on the shoulders with buttons and tied round the middle with either a matching belt or a fringed girdle, was supposed to be a regulation length. In most girls' schools a termly inspection involved each class kneeling on the floor of the gymnasium while the PE mistress, armed with a measuring stick, ensured that the gymslip was the requisite 4in off the ground. Woe betide the girl who tried to get away with a longer length by pushing out her chest and tucking up the back! Those wily PE teachers knew all the tricks.

Released from restrictions and geared up for a market ready for change, factories were producing not only a plentiful supply of ready-to-wear clothes for the shops but also the basic materials needed to make them. Rolls of cottons, silk, satin, taffeta and fine woollen cloth now filled the shelves of drapery departments in large stores throughout the country, their producers well aware that they would have a ready market amongst the women of this country who had learned to sew in times of need. Now, instead of having to turn a blanket into a winter coat, there

. . . our young 1950s wife would have worn both a hat and gloves when she went out.

would be the opportunity to buy beautiful tweed to make the coat of one's dreams. And those dreams were fostered by the manufacturers of paper patterns. How many young women whiled away a Saturday afternoon in a department store, leafing through those enormous glossy pattern books produced by Butterick, McCalls, Simplicity and Vogue.

This was the period when at last British women could share in the new materials that had been readily available to the American market – materials that had been developed in a chemistry laboratory, often as an offshoot of some other research. The 1950s housewife was familiar with nylon – or at least with the stockings which went by that name – but it would not be long before she would be wearing lingerie and nightwear made of nylon and then sleeping on nylon sheets. It was only a step or two to the introduction of brushed nylon, which, with the emergence of the company known as Brentford Nylons which had a store in most areas of the country, appeared to be taking over the whole domestic scene.

The more one looks at the fashions of the 1950s the more the word 'elegant' comes to mind. It was now possible for everyone to dress well for a reasonable price. Once cotton, for example, had been treated so that it was easy to wash and needed little ironing to retain its freshness, summer dresses in particular were a joy to behold. A young woman who possessed a couple of 'Horrockes' dresses was well set up to go anywhere, and if she was prepared to make her own then she could have more than two. The only problem was deciding which design to choose. By the mid-1950s, these cotton dresses, still calf length with a tightly belted waistline, had billowing skirts supported by either paper nylon or stiffened underskirts.

To complete her outfit, our young 1950s wife would have worn both a hat and gloves when she went out. For summer the hat would have been close fitting: a Juliet-style cap, or a simple stiffened band some 5in or 6in wide in a material that matched or toned with the dress. Both the new queen and her sister, Princess Margaret, were as much fashion leaders to copy as were film actresses like Grace

Kelly, Doris Day, Marilyn Monroe, Audrey Hepburn and Leslie Caron. Gloves were considered much more than simply items to keep your hands warm in winter. The 1950s women had been brought up by mothers who considered that 'no lady left the house without her gloves on – not put on as she walked down the street – but put on in the hall before she checked in the hall mirror that she was fit to face the world!' So gloves were worn all the year round. In summer these might be white or light-coloured wristlength items in nylon or thin cotton or possibly crocheted. If one was attending a special function such as a wedding or garden party, and your outfit had very short sleeves, then one would wear long gloves that stretched beyond the elbow. Long gloves were also worn with evening dresses, which were no longer the prerogative of the upper classes, but featured in the 1950s wardrobe for occasions such as the firm's Christmas dinner dance.

Again it was the women's magazines that came to the young woman's aid in showing her not only what was fashionable but also how she could, with 'a few deft touches

THE TIME TO LOOK AHEAD

GOOD LOOKS AND COMFORT COMBINE IN THESE THREE DESIGNS

DON'T you like a dress which can be made to look "different"? Bestway Dress Pattern No. D 3431 is cut on well-tried lines but has an unusual collar through which a gay scarf can be slotted to ring the changes.

USE a delicate floral print for the soft lines of Bestway Dress Pattern No. E 2502. There are many fabrics to choose from and they emphasize perfectly the femininity of the gathered bodice and gently billowing skirt.

HERE is a dress that is simple to slip into, and as fresh as a spring breeze. The bodice of Bestway Dress Pattern No. D 3876 is spiced with a neat strap which continues into the skirt and is fitted with sprung darts.

BESTWAY PATTERN No. D 3431 Price 2/9

(including postage and packing.) Cut in bust/hip sizes 36/40, 38/42, 40/44, 42/46, 44/48 and 48/52 inches.

BESTWAY PATTERN No. E 2502 Price 2/7

(including postage and packing.) Cut in bust/hip sizes 32/36, 34/38, 36/40, 38/42 and 40/44 inches.

BESTWAY PATTERN No. D 3876 Price 2/9

(including postage and packing.) Cut in bust/hip sizes 32/36, 34/38, 36/40, 38/42 and 40/44 inches.

D 3876. In 36-inch material allow 4¼ to 4½ yards or 4 to 4½ yards with short sleeves.

These Paper Patterns are obtainable only by post and NOT from any shop or store. Orders should be addressed to WOMAN'S WEEKLY Paper Pattern Department, P.O. Box 653, 21, Whitefriars Street, London, E.C.4.

Write, giving the Pattern Number, and please don't forget to state the bust size required. Money should be sent by Postal Order made payable to The Amalgamated Press, Ltd., and crossed " & Co." Overseas readers can obtain delivery of these patterns by mail from our London Pattern Dept. at the stated prices.

(centre) E 2502. Allow 4 to 4½ yards of 36-inch width or 4½ to 4¾ yards with ¾-sleeves.

(left) D 3431. Allow 4½ to 5½ yards of 36-inch width material.

Dress patterns in 1959. *Courtesy of Woman's Weekly*

give new life to many of the old-timers Further hints for updating included removing the collar from a suit jacket and changing the neckline into the more fashionable boat shape. At the same time the bottom hem could be turned up to fit just below the waist. If the jacket had a round neck it was suggested that this could be cut more deeply and the jacket could be worn over a high-necked jersey. To complete the renovation it was essential to cut off the cuffs, making the sleeves three-quarter length so that they 'will not get in the way at your desk'.

For the women who could afford a new dress for the spring, three patterns were advertised as being available from the magazine for around 2s 9d each. Two were obviously intended for the younger woman: both emphasised the nipped-in waist and billowing skirt. Unlike knitting patterns, these dresses were available in bust sizes from 32in to 40in and required between 4yds to 5yds of 36in-width material, which was a common width for most material at that time. The third design was for the more mature figure and was described as 'being cut on well tried lines' with soft pleats falling from the waist. However, an

attempt had been made to make this well-known design more up to date by offering 'a novel feature' – which turned out to be 'an unusual collar through which a gay [that is, a brightly coloured] scarf could be slotted to ring the changes'. This pattern started at bust size 36 and went right up to 48 and needed between 4¼yds to 5¼yds of material. Each of the women modelling these patterns was wearing a hat.

Of course, our woman did not totter out into the street either barefoot or in her bedroom slippers, for the 1950s witnessed a boom in the shoe industry too. From the sensible court shoe with a 1in to 1½in heel, this was the period of slender high heels and very narrow pointed-toed 'winkle-pickers', as the male version was known.

Many women suffered the acute embarrassment of becoming stuck when their heel sank right through someone's precious lino. Yet Mrs and Miss 1950s continued to force their feet into these shiny patent leather shoes, which came in vivid greens, reds and yellows – such a relief after years of black or brown – giving little thought to the corns and bunions they might suffer in later years. Having bought their shoes, a new handbag was needed. Bags at that time tended to be fairly small and compact, either a clutch type or box-like with a small carrying handle. The large shoulder bag would have been too reminiscent of a school satchel or, at worst, a gas-mask case, although those who needed to carry a lot with them might choose a leather bucket bag. However the majority of our women did not require a large bag as they carried little beyond a purse and a small make-up pouch, a clean hankie and the door key. No mobile telephone, no chequebook, no car keys, no wallet for credit cards … how did they manage?

There was a time when, as one walked along a street, usually of Victorian or Edwardian houses, one might spot a small brass plate situated beside the front door. Beautifully polished each day, these plates contained a finely etched name followed by a series of letters, discreetly advertising that this was the home and workplace of a dental surgeon or a music teacher. But gone is the brass plate that used to state 'Spirella Corsetier'. Inquisitive children who enquired the meaning of these words were usually fobbed off with 'that's nothing to do with you' or worse, 'you don't need to know about such things', which made it all the more intriguing. But, of course, your mother would not have wished to discuss details of such personal items as made-to-measure corsetry. There were already old established drapers' shops which specialised in ladies' lingerie and that also offered made-to-measure corsetry. But the independent Spirella corsetier must have been an early form of franchising. Like so many other companies, Spirella had started in the United States but, in Britain, was established in Letchworth, where suitable ladies were trained in the delicate art of selling as well as measuring clients for foundation garments. They could either work from their own homes or make visits to the client. They themselves wore the company's corsetry and displayed in their own figures the power of the garments to produce a sleek line under one's clothes. Emphasis was laid upon the importance of wearing a correctly fitted brassiere and keeping one's stomach under proper control. Women who had worn corsets during the 1940s believed that their daughters should be corseted too and many a slightly plump girl found herself in her teens being forced into an all-embracing form of pink or peach boned and laced armour plating that was totally embarrassing for the modern schoolgirl, who had not only to change for gym lessons but strip off all her clothes for showers. But not for long! Her mother and aunts might continue to keep the corset makers in business, but young Mrs 1950s was likely to buy her modern underwear over the counter at Marks & Spencer.

It was during the 1950s that the St Michael brand of underwear sold at Marks & Spencer covered the bodies of most of the women in this country. Quickly building up a reputation for well-made, fashionable and inexpensive garments, it became the shop from which young Mrs

> . . . bras and knickers offered a choice of the dainty, pretty flimsy ones to the down-to-earth white cotton ones that could be given a good boil.

1950s bought her nighties and pyjamas, both the thick winter winceyette variety as well as the trendy cotton, short-trouser ones known as baby dolls. Petticoats became known as slips, and bras and knickers offered a choice of the dainty, pretty flimsy ones to the down-to-earth white cotton ones that could be given a good boil.

Mrs or Miss 1950s also bought her suspender belts in Marks and if she needed to hold in the flab with more support than a suspender belt afforded, then she was offered a lightweight elasticated girdle, or roll-on, which came complete with suspenders, which of course were necessary for holding up your stockings. And so we move to the hosiery counter, where one had a choice of stockings. Strange now to think that stockings were bought according to one's shoe size and that once upon a time the best were made either of silk or nylon and were fashioned on the shape of a leg. The seamed variety had little flashings which indicated they were 'fully fashioned' so the seam fell comfortably into place on the back of the leg. The sheer silk ones, like the early nylons, were easily snagged with a fingernail and there was nothing worse than going

> . . . there was nothing worse than going somewhere special and discovering that a ladder had appeared in your stocking.

somewhere special and discovering that a ladder had appeared in your stocking. First-aid treatment consisted of rubbing a dampened piece of soap just under the end of the run in an effort to stop it going any further. A more drastic method was to apply a dab of colourless nail varnish on it. The drawback here was that it could stick the stocking to your leg. If one wanted to emphasise the back seam, one wore the stockings inside out; this was considered to be eye-catching and thus more attractive. Apart from fine

silk, there was also rayon, which was slightly more hard-wearing, but the strongest of all was lisle. However, lisle stockings lacked stretchiness and, being the stockings worn by senior girls at school, were promptly rejected by our young housewives, who probably still had memories of that awful gap between the top of the stocking and underwear, especially noticeable when riding a bicycle in wintertime. The idea that one day she would be pulling on an all-in-one nylon garment that resembled a pair of elongated, shapeless bags grafted on to a larger one that came up to her waist would have been quite incomprehensible as well as seen as totally unhygienic.

During the 1940s, trousers had, for many women, become part of their working clothes. These were very different to the smart, well-cut linen trousers that had featured in the years leading up to the war, and that tended to be worn by what was termed 'the smart set'. Newsreel pictures at the cinema showed Mrs Simpson looking elegant in them; betrousered film stars relaxed on board yachts; and in romantic comedies bright young things

wore theirs at weekend country-house parties where they drank cocktails. This was far removed from the life of the average working woman and, in a moralistic age, there was still something 'not quite right' about a woman wearing trousers. So although they were considered fashionable in America it took time for slacks to become widely accepted in Britain. Some men who disapproved of the practice actually forbade their wives to wear them. Others would countenance their being worn for leisure activities such as cycling or hiking or for working round the home. Women too were often reluctant to be tempted into trousers even when they saw how attractive one could look in designs that had a high waist, side zips and a flat front panel, which emphasised a slim figure. Jeans did not arrive on the scene until towards the end of the 1950s. Having been made popular by James Dean in *Rebel Without a Cause*, they were adopted by the emerging teen culture, so again, not really the thing for a housewife.

Once the restrictions on materials had been relaxed, designers were able to be more imaginative in the styles of that which was essential to every woman's wardrobe – the

winter coat. In those days, this was not an item one bought annually. It was still ingrained in many that one had a 'best coat'; that is, the new one, which was worn on Sundays and for special occasions Once your best coat had been cleaned a couple of times, it was time to move it to everyday use and take the plunge and buy a new one for best.

The designs of the 1950s varied from the double-breasted, brass-buttoned Cossack style in black, red or navy – most startling of all in white but not practical for day-to-day wear – which was extremely flattering to a slim figure. This coat, worn with a large fur hat, was bound to excite envy as well as comment. More down to earth was the swagger coat, with its very full swing-back and wrap-over buttonless front. A novel aspect of this design was that a matching tie belt was slotted through the small vent on either side of the waist and drawn round to hold the front in place. These coats came in two lengths, one just below the knee, the other ending on the thigh. Colours were either plain vivid reds, blues or greens, or the more startling huge multi-shaded blocks of the sort which nowadays might be found on a picnic rug.

... a fetching little cocktail hat might be worn for a drinks party.

This does not, however, explain why hats slowly went out of fashion generally for younger women. The 1950s bride almost always included a hat in her going-away outfit and the average woman still wore a hat for church on Sundays, in many cases still hanging on to the old tradition of buying a new one for Easter. Hats were still de rigueur for weddings and funerals, and if one moved in the right social circles then one definitely wore a hat for a luncheon engagement, while a fetching little cocktail hat might be worn for a drinks party. In the 1950s there were not only numerous small shops which specialised in ladies' millinery, but both Marks & Spencer and British Home Stores had counters close to the main entrance where hats for every season and all occasions were not only on display but could be picked up and tried on. There were even hand mirrors so that you could see from every angle how you looked. Many a 1950s woman whiled away a cold or wet Saturday afternoon trying on hats she had no intention of buying while her husband attended the local football match. But she might have been tempted, if the price was right – and it has to be said that hats were not beyond the purse of many. Of course,

At some stage most girls were given a pearl necklace.

for the woman who worked, and travelled in all weathers on her bicycle, a hat of some sort was a very necessary item. A knitted helmet type or pixie hood was ideal for winter wear and again magazines came to the rescue with instructions on how to make these.

Swiftly passing on from the naughty to the nice, the 1950s woman was offered a wide selection of adornments in the way of reasonably priced jewellery to complement her outfits. At some stage most girls were given a pearl necklace. This might be fashioned from the expensive real pearls or the less expensive cultured ones, or from those that were totally artificial. A pearl necklace was often given

as a 21st birthday present or a bride received one as a gift from her husband to wear on their wedding day. If this was the case, it is to be hoped that she was not superstitious. However, for some, pearls were now considered to be 'old-fashioned' – there was the terrible stigma of being seen wearing the 'old maid's' outfit of a cardigan and jumper twinset with a string of pearls, even though those young ladies who featured in the pages of *Country Life* magazine continued to display their precious family pearls. But then, those young debutantes were usually announcing their engagements, so they were all right.

For the general run of the female population, however, there was now a wide choice of new and exciting designs for necklaces, bracelets and earrings using rhinestones, diamanté and marcarsite, which came at an affordable price. Often it was possible to buy individual pieces over time to form a matching set. Then it became fashionable to wear large strings of coloured plastic beads known as 'poppits'. Each bead had a small projection that fitted into a matching small hole. No longer 'strung' on thread as was the conventional method with a necklace, the 'poppits' slotted one into the other and thus one could

Very few women then had their ears pierced.

shorten or lengthen the necklace at will or alternatively turn it into a number of bracelets to be worn at once. Other composite materials were used to produce chunky beads; it was particularly popular to wear graded white ones with summer dresses. One fashion that has changed radically since the 1950s is the decline in clip-on earrings. Very few women then had their ears pierced. The biggest drawback was that after a time the spring clip became slack and the earring would fall off, or if you forgot to remove them when undressing, they could easily get caught when you were pulling a dress or jumper over your head and get lost. What then to do with the one remaining? If it was of sufficient size and interest, then the enterprising woman might turn it into a scarf clip or use it on the collar of a dress or coat as a brooch.

For the woman who could not afford to buy jewellery this was the period of experiment and many tried their hand at creating their own. Many were the brooches made at this time, either by painting designs on to a clear plastic backing that held a fastener or by pouring plaster of Paris into moulds of various shapes – small dogs seemed the most popular – or creating sprays of delicate flowers from twisted plastic-covered wire. There were no limits to the creativity of the 1950s woman.

How many 1950s women had, as children, raided their mother's wardrobes for dressing up and been horrified to discover that a dead animal lurked there? It is hard now to imagine anyone placing a complete fox over her best Sunday costume and going off to church. The animal was placed over one's shoulder and fastened in place by a clip in the fox's mouth. It was in the 1950s that the farming of wild mink from America really took off and this was

responsible for providing most of the fur trade of the period. The 1950s woman who had been repelled by her mother wearing a whole dead fox was now quite happy to follow the fashion to have a mink collar on her winter coat and a matching mink hat and even little mink pompoms on her high-heeled shoes. If she was wealthy enough she might own a real fur stole to wear for evenings or social occasions. She might even have a full-length fur coat bought from a specialist furrier. Less expensive ones were available in the shops but buying one of those could lead to the abusive envy of one's neighbours.

8

Health and Beauty

The introduction of the National Health Service in 1948 gave every man, woman and child in the country the right of access to all forms of medical treatment, from a simple consultation with a general practitioner to hospital treatment that might involve an expensive and intricate operation, for free. To those who had in the past paid for their medical care through a small regular payment this was wonderful news indeed. Even better was the realisation that the doctor could now also write a prescription for free medicines, tablets and medical supplies. The new scheme also revolutionised the way the doctors held their surgeries. There had been a time when, if you were worried about someone's state of health, you either sent a message to the surgery – often held in part of the doctor's house – or you went to the nearest telephone box where you rang the doctor's number, reported the situation and invariably, at some time during the day, the doctor would make a visit to your home to examine the patient. However, once most people had registered with the doctor, as one was now obliged to do, the doctor had less time for home visits, which became limited to real emergencies. There was no

. . . she would persuade her invalid to sit with his head over the steaming bowl . . .

appointment system, you simply turned up and waited your turn, which might take anything up to an hour to come.

The 1950s housewife would have known that when her husband had a bad cold that involved severely congested nasal passages then the answer was to purchase a bottle of Friar's Balsam. Filling a bowl (often her yellow mixing bowl from the kitchen) with boiling water into which she placed a few drops of the powerful yellow mixture, she would persuade her invalid to sit with his head over the steaming bowl while she used a large towel to make a sort

of tent over his head so that he could clear the congestion by inhaling the strong fumes that rose up. Incidentally, the concentrated steaming was also good for opening the pores on the face if one happened to suffer with blackheads. The early 1950s housewife was also likely to treat a stye with Golden Eye ointment, and use zinc and castor oil ointment for rashes and boracic ointment for cuts and grazes. Germolene was also used for the latter purpose, although Dettol and TCP were far more fashionable, if more expensive, than common old salt and water for cleansing wounds, and less painful than iodine.

In the war years most families had kept a stock of old sheeting for home emergencies, and thin strips were torn off and rolled up ready to make bandages. In the days before sticky tape was in general use it was usual to split the end of the sheeting bandage down to the required length to make a self-tie. But by the 1950s, there were ample stocks not only of lint, which was placed over a wound, but proper bandages too, and sticking plasters which could supplant the use of the gauze bandages. The adhesive quality of these fabric plasters was much stronger than the later plasticized ones, as anyone who had one ripped off could testify. Removal by ripping intensified but shortened the pain.

The desire of women to be slim and youthful is nothing new – however far back in time one cares to go, you will find a method that was supposed to achieve miracles. In the 1950s advertisements appeared in women's magazines under the banner 'Figure it out' accompanied by a line drawing of an elegant woman in a smart suit and wearing a close-fitting hat adorned with two large feathers, one hand on her slim waist, the other on the head of a dog of the retriever type. The text read:

> . . . one of the oddest aids of shedding weight appeared during the second half of the 1950s . . .

You ARE young when you feel young ... you feel young when you LOOK young. Zest, poise, vitality – all the gaiety of a happy, full life – these make up the charm of the woman who preserves the girlish lines of youth.

How did one achieve this? By taking Marmola brand anti-fat tablets. At 3s 8½d a box, these were quite expensive. Like most of the articles of this type that appeared in advertisements they were available from the chemist's or by post, so that they could be acquired discreetly.

Perhaps one of the oddest aids to shedding weight appeared during the second half of the 1950s in the shape, no pun intended, of Stephanie Bowman slimming garments. The term garment was somewhat misleading for what in fact amounted to a series of pink plastic bags with elasticated tops and bottoms. Working on the principle of a Turkish bath, the idea was that you could reduce certain areas of your body by encasing the part – thighs and upper arms in particular – in one of the bags and then wearing one's clothes over the top either all

night or during the day. The resulting sweat was supposed to start the slimming process.

For the occasional headache or stomach cramps the 1950s housewife would have taken Aspros, which were sold individually encased in strips of pink paper. Phensic, which was advertised as being better than aspirin alone, was also popular, and was offered as a remedy for a variety of ailments including rheumatic pains, while by the middle to end of the decade both codeine and Anadin tablets were on the market. Codeine was used widely in a number of medicines for its analgesic qualities but its use was eventually curtailed when its addictive quality was recognised. During the 1950s great strides were made in the pharmaceutical industry that led to the introduction of tablets being used in various treatments; two important ones were penicillin and the mysteriously named M & B tablets. You knew you had something rather special if the doctor said, 'I'll put you on M & B'.

Since we have just toured the chemist's shop and in passing have mentioned menstruation, which was rarely mentioned publicly, this seems the appropriate place to talk of the sanitary products available in the 1950s. Bulky sanitary towels, packed by the dozen in almost plain wrappers were purchased either from an old-fashioned drapery shop or from the chemist. For the young woman it was embarrassing to have to ask the male chemist for a packet of Lilia or Silcot. In the 1950s it was a brave unmarried woman who dared to ask for a packet of Tampax or Lillets, for many women there was a fear that they might somehow harm themselves by using internal protection, while it was believed by some that it was impossible for an unmarried woman – that is, a presumed virgin – to be capable of using them. It often took an enlightened female PE teacher to explain that school gymnastics had taken care of that particular concern.

One thing has become apparent during the last fifty years and that is that the longer we live, the younger we seem to remain. For a start, women are no longer expected to 'dress their age', whatever that means, but there was a

. . . by the time you had reached 50 you were expected to settle for what can only be described as downright dowdy clothes.

time when fashions were produced with certain age groups in mind. Designers for the mass market produced garments that were aimed at the younger woman, 'the junior Miss', who was about to start work, and those in their 20s; next came the more mature woman, and by the time you had reached 50 you were expected to settle for what can only be described as downright dowdy clothes. Think Ena Sharples and her friends. Similarly, clothes were sized: 'W' (Women), 'WX' (Women's Extra) and 'OS' (Outsize). Manufacturers tended to assume that as women aged so they expanded in size, so the more stylish dresses were in W size and the more matronly were WX or OS. This was extremely hard on the young woman who was not stock size and was forced to find something to fit her from the outsize range. There were few words more humiliating than 'I'm afraid we have nothing in your size, Madam!' On the subject of sizing, while today we have some women striving to achieve a one-digit size, others are much bigger than they were in the 1950s. The knitting patterns of the era were for a standard bust size of 34/35in and 36/37in. Only occasionally did they extend as far as the larger size of 39/40.

. . . the rouge that mother had used was definitely consigned to the back of the dressing table drawer.

Pond's had held the market in face cream for a long time; many a school child had been mystified by the advertisement for its Vanishing Cream. Certainly most 1950s housewives would have started using it, even if in time they moved on to other products. But it was inexpensive and had a proven record, and was a good base for the requisite application of face powder. An essential item in every woman's handbag was her powder compact. A girl knew that she had truly reached womanhood when she was presented with one of these; often given as a really expensive 21st birthday present. Varying in shape as well as material, invariably the design on the lid was inlaid with painted or enamel flowers or birds. Inside the lid was a mirror, then came the small powder puff, beneath which was the insert through which the powder was filtered. In those days loose face powder was sold in small round boxes from which one filled the compact. In many ways this was both messy and time consuming, so the arrival of compressed powder refills was warmly welcomed.

Then came pancake make-up introduced by Max Factor, as an offshoot of that used in films. Eyeshadow and eyebrow pencils were used to highlight the eyes, while

the rouge that mother had used was definitely consigned to the back of the dressing table drawer. The introduction of pale shimmering pink for both lipstick and nail varnish widened the customer base as many young women whose parents and later husbands had believed that bright red lips and nails were not for the likes of them dared to try the pinks.

It is difficult nowadays to imagine what it was like before the days of self-service in practically every store. With counters and display cases manned by assistants, one really needed to know what it was you wanted to purchase. Fortunately, for Miss and Mrs Average, there was always Woolworths, which kept a good range of cosmetics on show as well as reasonably priced perfumes, the most popular of which was Bourjois Evening in Paris, with its distinctive dark blue bottles and packaging.

Ladies in the past had kept cut-glass, silver-topped bowls on their dressing tables filled with dusting powder but by the 1950s the perfume makers were producing fancy tins of talcum powder available to every woman. These tins, teamed up with perfumed soap (now no longer rationed), and placed in a fancy box became ideal Christmas gifts. Often the box also contained either a bottle of coloured bath salts (scented washing-soda crystals) or half a dozen bath cubes. These squares, about the size of four Oxo cubes, wrapped in silver paper with an outer wrapper that declared what scent they were, were crumbled – just like the Oxo or a Symington's soup cube – into one's bath. Bath salts were also sold loose by weight and the enterprising woman could practice both economy and recycling by filling jam jars, which she had previously decorated, with the bath crystals. For a few pence and a little time and skill, she had achieved several presents for female family and friends.

Towards the end of the 1950s, we were becoming much more concerned about how we smelled – or didn't, as the case might be. The makers of Lifebuoy soap had made us all aware of its power to remove body odour, and advertisements began to appear suggesting that it was the duty of a best friend not to shirk telling one the truth. Although there was an old saying that 'horses sweat, gentlemen perspire and ladies glow', our housewives too were now regularly using underarm deodorants. To begin with, some of these came in liquid form, like Odo-o-no, or as a cream, like Arrid, before developing into roll-ons and aerosol spray anti-perspirants. If they could stand the smell housewives were also removing the hair on their legs and underarms with Veet – a practice best done when husbands were out of the house.

For the girls who as children had cleaned their teeth after rubbing a dampened toothbrush on the little solid pink block known as dentifrice, manufactured by Gibbs

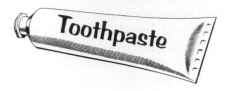

and sold in small red tins bearing what we would now call a logo of little ivory towers, there was now not only a choice of toothpaste but mouthwashes too to make sure that their breath was always 'fresh'.

The great beauty debate that has raged for generations of whether or not to wash one's face with soap and water was still going on in the 1950s even though by then toilet soap no longer contained the harsh elements of the past. Lux, for example, boasted of its purity and gentleness upon the skin, as did other well-known brands such as Imperial Leather and Palmolive. But this was the era when products appeared on the market that proved just how useless soap

> Her lifestyle was such that she took plenty of exercise without even thinking about it.

and water were in cleansing the skin. One lotion instructed you to dab it all over the face and then remove it bit by bit with small pads of cotton wool. When one saw the dirt that was removed, it would be months, if ever, before one reverted to soap and water. This was also the era of blackheads that needed to be steamed and gently squeezed to remove them. And, of course, there was always the face pack – preferably one that contained yeast. It was essential that the young housewife had time and privacy to plaster her face with the white mixture which not only caused all the pores in the face to open but, when it set hard, was supposed to tighten all one's facial muscles. Absolute stillness was required during this treatment; woe betide anyone who disturbed the recipient, causing the mask to crack. Once it was well and truly set, then came the messy operation of washing it all off. Then it was time to lie down and relax with a slice of cucumber placed on each eyelid.

The 1950s housewife would have been very keen to maintain a healthy weight. Her lifestyle was such that she took plenty of exercise without even thinking about it. She automatically walked daily to the shops to buy fresh food, or to work; or, if the latter was several miles away, she would cycle. Her work within the house also involved more energy than the modern housewife expends. Laundry done by hand involved filling bowls or tubs, rubbing the items, wringing the garments and finally walking out with the laundry basket to the garden and hanging it out on the line. Similarly, not everyone had a vacuum cleaner so floors were swept and polished, carpets brushed and kitchen floors scrubbed. Windows were regularly cleaned inside and out, though fortunately the disappearance of sash windows brought an end to the practice of the housewife sitting on the window sill to clean the outside of upper-storey windows. Many women continued to play tennis or netball, while the popular Saturday night dance still provided splendid exercise. And, of course, there was always the gardening to be done.

The 1950s woman had grown up accustomed to the limited diet enforced by rationing, thus she had not been able to indulge a 'sweet tooth' with a never-ending supply of confectionery, cakes and biscuits. Both finance and the routine of three meals a day with the occasional treat conditioned what she ate. But, of course, there were some who thought they needed to lose weight, and these women were advised to follow a regime that cut out carbohydrates, which in those days meant bread and potatoes. The more recent cabbage soup diet was preceded by that of the cauliflower, where the cooking liquor was drunk first, the cauliflower head forming the main meal.

Bathroom scales were not in general use in the 1950s, so if one was trying to watch one's weight, it was necessary to use the scales in your local chemist's shop. The most accurate were those where weights were moved across

a beam placed in front of you. To get a really accurate reading, you needed the chemist or his assistant to move the weights along the beam. If, however, you did not wish to reveal your weight to anyone else, then you could, for the price of one penny in the slot, be weighed by standing on a small platform, and your weight would be recorded on the dial in front of you. If you were a glutton for punishment, then you took your penny to Woolworths and stood on the scales, which were usually situated just inside the main entrance. This gigantic red machine had an enormous dial and once you stood on the platform your weight was revealed to the world at large.

While on the subject of placing pennies in the slot, in the 1950s the now euphemistic term for visiting the lavatory really did mean spending a penny. Perhaps we can include this under the heading of health – that is, public health. In the 1950s every town had a number of public lavatories placed at regular intervals to ensure that one was never far from a convenience. Often these were placed in or near bus stations or trolley bus termini and were situated below ground where they might also provide an area where parcels could be left while doing one's shopping. Male and female facilities were rarely placed side by side; they were situated instead at a discreet distance. In the majority of cases, the lavatories were supervised by attendants, who took a pride in keeping their domain spotless. Not only were the cubicles kept clean and polished but, in those days when the water supply to the overhead cisterns was carried in copper pipes, these glowed like beacons, betokening the attendant's pride in his or her work. Each cubicle had a slot machine on its door and it was into this that you placed your penny. Some conveniences had one cubicle tucked

... a deterrent to those who delighted in writing rhymes and messages on the cubicle walls ...

away that was free, for the use of those who were needy. However, something which would appal today's health and safety inspectors was that in those days there were no general handwashing facilities. You could, if you wished, pay sixpence for what was called a wash and brush up. The lavatory attendant would take your money and provide you with some soap and a towel, then admit you to an inner sanctum beyond a glass door. Here there were several washbasins that provided hot water. There was also a mirror for the lady to repair her make-up. A small but prominent little dish on the attendant's table, which might include another with safety pins or a needle and thread, indicated that a small tip would be appreciated.

Some councils decided to dispense with the penny in the slot on the cubicle doors and instead installed turnstiles at the entrance into which the penny was inserted. This was often a reaction to beat the petty criminals who attempted to break open the machine on the cubicle door. It was also intended as a deterrent to those who delighted in writing rhymes and messages on the cubicle walls or who used unsupervised lavatories as a meeting place.

However, turnstiles caused very serious problems for some members of the public. The first was that you had to have the requisite coin for the slot. With the old method, the attendant was able to give you change. With a turnstile, a desperate person might have to wait for some time to find another prospective user who would either give them a penny or change the larger coin. There was a joke at the time that the definition of a gentleman was one who, when asked for a penny, did not give two halfpennies. But the biggest drawback to the turnstile for women involved size. To start with a mother with a baby in a pushchair was unable to get that through; if she had a toddler there could be problems trying to squeeze the child through with her. The heavy iron framework was enough to frighten a small child from ever using one again. Elderly and disabled women also had problems, but those who suffered most were those who did not conform to the size allocated by the mechanism to allow entry. By the late 1950s the plight of all women in the use of turnstiles was discussed at great length in parliament, the cause being taken up initially by Barbara Castle, backed by the larger-than-life MP Bessie Braddock. Finally, in 1963, turnstiles in public lavatories provided by local authorities were made illegal.

9

The Status of Women

The official view of the status of married women in the 1950s is summed up neatly in the word 'housewife'. After the war, when demobilised servicemen returned to take up their old work, women were no longer needed to do the jobs they had held down during the men's absence and the powers that be decided that one of the ways to deal with this and build a new, better Britain was by creating the nuclear family with the wife/mother set securely in the centre of the home, rather as the middle classes had done in late Victorian times. Worthy though this idea might be, it generated an attitude in many workplaces that since young women employees were not likely to stay long in a job once they were married, because inevitably they would start a family, it was not worth giving them any extra training that would set them on the path to a successful career. Carrying this policy to its logical conclusion meant that many women who remained unmarried, or married but childless, were denied the opportunities for promotion they should have had. To combat this prejudice young engaged women in teacher-training colleges were often warned they should not wear their rings when attending an interview for a post. However, in those pre-'politically

... the perfect stay-at-home housewife who took care of the home ...

correct days', the governing body and members of the interview panel could ask any questions they liked, even if it did come occasionally dressed up in the euphemism of the gentleman who asked a candidate, 'Miss ..., are you, um, so to speak, heart-whole and fancy free?' Worse perhaps, was the interview panel who turned down a well-qualified candidate for a head of department position on the grounds that, newly married at the ripe old age of 30, she would be bound to start a family almost immediately.

Books, magazines, films and, later, television programmes tried hard to reinforce the idyllic picture of the perfect stay-at-home housewife who took care of the home, raised the children, cooked nutritious meals, and provided a haven of calm for her hardworking husband when he returned at the end of his working day. The romantic novelist Barbara Cartland was often to be heard on the wireless dispensing advice on how the good wife should prepare herself to greet her husband, not only with a delicious meal prepared but herself bathed, perfumed and dressed in smart clean clothes, complete with fresh frilly apron, ready to spend a cosy and possibly romantic evening with him. One wonders how many frazzled women were

tempted to throw something at the radio after they had spent the day wrestling with a fractious, teething baby and a 2-year-old's tantrums, not to mention the broken washing line that had trailed all the clean nappies in the flowerbeds. They would, of course, have their husband's evening meal ready but it was doubtful if they would have had the time to run a comb through their hair, let alone wash their face and apply make-up. The women who might take Miss Cartland's advice or heed that given in magazines were those who most probably had some help in the house. If all your washing went to the laundry from whence everything, including your husband's shirts, returned beautifully ironed, and if you had an obliging Mrs Mopp who came, perhaps not every day but certainly more than once a week, to scrub, clean and polish, then like Mrs Dale whose diary was broadcast daily, you too could strive to be the perfect housewife.

However, the reality for most women was very different. Most of the young couples who married during the 1950s relied on saving the wife's weekly wage towards furnishing their home, or providing necessities for when they started a family. The younger the husband the more likely he was to accept that his wife worked, and often he was prepared to share the household chores with her. Older husbands were more entrenched in their outlook – as, it would seem, were some of those who lived in the countryside. These were likely to adopt the attitude of, 'No wife of mine is going out to work!' Whether this was from fear that other people would think him incapable of providing adequately for her or an unconscious desire to retain his control of her is not clear. The wife who remained at home was wholly dependent on her husband for money. If one belonged to the more affluent parts of society then the husband might make his wife a monthly allowance for her own personal use – no questions asked. He would probably also take responsibility for all the household bills. On the other hand, the majority of stay-at-home wives were given a sum from their husband's weekly pay packet and were expected to run the house, and feed and clothe themselves and later the children, out of it. In some households the man handed over his unopened pay packet to his wife who then gave

> **Most stay-at-home wives had a set amount given to them that was considered sufficient to buy the weekly food supplies.**

him back what amounted to his pocket money. Others allotted varying amounts into tins or jars to cover the rent, bills for the utilities, insurance policies or to pay the regular installments on essential items, such as the gas or electric cooker, bought on a hire-purchase agreement. Another receptacle was earmarked for storing the one-, later two-shilling pieces needed to feed the gas and electricity meters if that method of payment was used.

The most haphazard of all these financial arrangements was the one where the husband placed his wages in a disused teapot or caddy on the mantelpiece, most usually, or on the top shelf of the kitchen cupboard. This 'bank' was then drawn on when needed but it was a method that relied on great trust that neither party would be tempted to overspend on some non-essential item. Most stay-at-home wives had a set amount given to them that was considered sufficient to buy the weekly food supplies. Whichever system was adopted, it was left to the housewife to squirrel away what she could, to cover such items as make-up, a rare visit to the hairdresser, or birthday and Christmas presents.

This dependency or being viewed merely as an adjunct to one's husband overlapped into other areas. For a

A wife's salary, however large it was, could not be counted towards a mortgage.

married woman who also worked, there was nothing more annoying, when faced with an official form that required the answer to the question 'occupation' to be instructed by the official on the other side of the desk or counter, to write 'housewife'. And worse, being told that you needed your husband's permission, verified by his signature, to do certain things, such as enter into a hire-purchase agreement. It was assumed that a woman might default on payments, unless they were backed by her husband. A wife's salary, however large it was, could not, for example, be counted towards a mortgage. However, unmarried women with a decent salary were able to obtain a mortgage provided it was adequately backed by a life insurance policy. As a single woman one could sign legal documents and was considered intelligent enough both to understand and negotiate with builders, agents and solicitors. But as a married woman things were very different; every little detail had to be passed and signed for by her new husband, which, as he was often working away, could prove difficult. It is hardly surprising that during the 1950s feminism was bubbling away below the surface.

One fight that was on going during the 1950s was for equal pay for women and men doing the same or similar jobs. Women teachers and civil servants achieved parity by the end of the 1950s but other employers took much more convincing and women continued to be paid less than their male counterparts. Similarly, women were still not readily accepted in what were considered male professions. The first female bank manager was appointed in 1958 but even after this momentous event, many older managers refused to appoint female counter assistants. Worse perhaps than this chauvinistic attitude on the part of the manager was the hostility of some of the male customers who, when women did appear behind the counter, refused to be served by them and would deliberately move to a counter served by a male. If it was hard for some men to accept women working in banks, how much more tenacity would a bright girl who wanted to be an engineer need; first to persuade her teachers so that she could study the right subjects to gain the relevant place at university and, having gained that place, often with great difficulty, and then achieved a good degree, to find an engineering company that would take her on. Slowly, slowly, graduates in mathematics and all the sciences

broke down barriers and opened the way for others, but very often not without a fight for acceptance and equality.

Women were supposed to stay at home and look after the children. They were expected to be pure and chaste, whereas a man might have been lonely during the war. It was accepted that men would have dalliances but where a man could walk away from his entanglements, a woman was sometimes literally left holding the baby.

If this happened, and there was no way the wife could pretend her husband was the father, then he had one of the few grounds for divorce that were available at that time. Again, it was a class thing. Readers of the Sunday newspapers were kept abreast of the activities of those in the higher echelons of society whose marriages were dissolved, often involving large financial settlements. American film stars also went off to the city of Reno where, according to the gossip columns, it was possible to get a 'quickie' divorce that would enable a new marriage to take place shortly afterwards. But divorce was not for ordinary people, not only because of the legal costs involved but also because of the stigma that accompanied such action. If a partner was found to

... those who lived apart for seven years should be granted a divorce without question.

have committed adultery then dissolution of the marriage might be considered. But, mainly because of the financial implications, it was more likely that a man would sue on the grounds of his wife's adultery than that she would take action against him, even if he was a serial adulterer. As the wife was financially dependent on her husband she was not in a position to leave the marital home and take the children with her, so many women stayed in abusive or utterly dead relationships because there was no alternative.

Amongst the more enlightened in government and elsewhere, there was an acknowledgement that the whole question of divorce needed modernising, so, in 1951, a Royal Commission was set up to consider a change in the laws which permitted divorce only on the grounds of matrimonial fault – adultery, cruelty – or desertion of three or more years. It was argued that marriage should no longer be regarded as a binding legal duty but rather a companionate union, and therefore if the relationship of love and affection broke down it should be terminated. It was also proposed that those who had lived apart for seven years should be granted a divorce without question. In 1956 there was a further Royal Commission on both marriage and divorce that recognised that many of our accepted standards had altered:

> [It has to be accepted] ... that greater demands are now made of marriage, consequent on the spread of education, higher standards of living and the social and economic emancipation of women ... Old restraints, such as social penalties on sexual relations outside marriage, have weakened ... [and there is] a tendency to regard the assertion of one's own individuality as a right and to pursue one's personal satisfaction, reckless of the consequences to others ... There is a tendency to take the duties and responsibilities of marriage less seriously than formerly.

It is interesting to see that what, sixty years later, has been dubbed as the 'Me' generation obviously had its seeds in the 1950s. Recognising that life had changed was one thing but taking action was another. The Commission and the government still saw marriage as an institution not a

relationship. Therefore adultery was an offence against an institution, which harmed the moral and social fabric of society. Thus the wrongdoer should be punished. So strongly did they feel on the subject they actually considered abolishing divorce altogether. Better, they believed, to educate the nation on the duties and responsibilities of marriage – something they are still talking about in the second decade of the twenty-first century. So nothing further was done to help those who wished to extricate themselves from difficult marriages until the matter came up again for review in the 1960s. Thus a number of women had to endure not only the torment of a loveless marriage but also had to put up with the disapproval of their parents and families at the very mention of a divorce.

Many women gave up their own ambitions for a good career and took less fulfilling jobs merely to earn money that would help them if their husbands were studying. There were those young men who had left school at 15, gone to work and then been conscripted to do their two years' National Service, who discovered that they had no wish to return to their previous dead-end employment but

wished instead to better their chances in life. Some chose to follow a different career path entirely, which would require additional study to achieve their aim. Thousands of young wives supported their husbands financially as they attended short-term college courses, while for those undertaking home-study or evening courses, the additional expense of textbooks and fees was drawn from the wife's pay packet. Times were indeed hard for these couples but the experience seems to have strengthened rather than weakened their relationships.

10

Let's Talk About Sex

Those who are in the habit of picking up a book and reading the last chapter first may be somewhat taken aback by the rather blunt heading to this chapter, for sex was one subject that was rarely mentioned in polite company. It was almost as if it did not exist. There was a joke in the 1950s that was partly a criticism of the affected speech of certain parts of society at the time who would insist on pronouncing 'a' as 'e', that ran along the lines that 'sex is what the poor people have their coal delivered in!' It had always been accepted that the upper classes had quite different standards to the other classes. Everyone had either met or read about someone who was the illegitimate offspring of a poor misused servant girl and the 'lord of the manor', but they didn't talk about that anymore than they talked about 'mistakes' that may have happened in their own families, especially in wartime. On the whole, the majority of the nation regarded 'making love' or sexual intercourse as something to be conducted in the privacy,

and possibly darkness, of one's bedroom and therefore of no concern to anyone else. The word 'intercourse' often appeared in reports of notable divorce cases in Sunday newspapers such as the *News of the World*. Any intelligent child who avidly read whatever was available and used a dictionary too was likely to grin during school assembly when confronted with the hymn that spoke of a 'closer intercourse with Him'. Ironically, in this free, liberated twenty-first century we still use the euphemistic phrase, 'sleeping together' even though practically every primary school child is well aware that sleeping is not the main activity involved.

This is not the place to delve into either the religious influences or the deep-seated psychological reasons why parents in the past were so reluctant to talk to their children about procreation. Suffice it to say that in the 1950s most girls had gained what they knew about sex from their schoolfellows; quite where they got their information from was never made clear. Some girls' schools, however, actually tackled the vital question of how a baby was made by dealing with it in a biology lesson:

We knew from the girls in the year above that when we got to the Rabbit lesson, all would be revealed. When the day came we had a young biology teacher who was due to marry at the end of term, so that made it all the more exciting. We spent part of the lesson drawing the cross section of the rabbit's interior organs in our notebooks and labelling different parts of its anatomy. But it was getting close to the end of the lesson and we still hadn't got to the part we were waiting for. Finally, a very pink Miss explained the copulation of rabbits. The bell rang for the end of the lesson. She picked up her books and made for the lab door, turned and said 'And the same thing applies to human beings!' And that was all the sex education we had in our Grammar School!

Even those who knew all the facts were not always prepared for the strong emotions that physical love could arouse both in themselves and their partner. Many girls started their married lives entirely unprepared for what lay ahead

of them on their wedding night. Some mothers didn't give them any advice or guidance, merely hinting with some embarrassment at what might happen; sometimes suggesting, perhaps as a result of their own experience, that it would be a painful experience that had to be endured. Other mothers – and occasionally mothers-in-law – would casually leave a book or a leaflet in a bedside drawer that contained helpful information in preparation for the wedding night. At least the bride-to-be whose mother gave her a copy of Marie Stopes' book *Married Love* to read had more practical guidance to help her.

Despite their lack of knowledge and experience most contributors reported that they quickly settled into a satisfying sex life with their husbands. Time and time again they reported how gentle and supportive their husbands had been. Initially, once a couple had decided that either for financial or housing reasons they did not wish to start a family immediately, it was the husband who took the necessary precautions to prevent conception. In this age of sexual liberation it is difficult to comprehend what it was like in the 1950s when contraception was acknowledged but not encouraged, certainly not by some branches of the

Church. Contraceptives came in the form of condoms, then mostly called by their nicknames of French letters or rubber johnnies, or simply by the trade name of Durex. These were not on display anywhere. A visit to the barber's shop by a young man might elicit the discreet enquiry as he paid for his haircut, 'do you require anything for the weekend, Sir?' If the answer was in the affirmative, then the little packets were produced. Otherwise the only other supplier was the chemist. Again, the man couldn't just select what he wanted and pay for it – he had to ask! The items would then be produced from under the counter, almost like a black market packet of biscuits. It took courage for a young man, even though now married, to ask a female assistant in the chemist's shop for what he wanted and often he would hang around staring into glass display cabinets until he could approach the male chemist.

Condoms were not 100 per cent reliable and perhaps, after the scare of an unwanted pregnancy or where it was

> 'married people may space
> or limit their families
> and thus might mitigate
> the evils of ill health and
> poverty'.

decided that a family must definitely be postponed, the woman took responsibility for contraception. Generations before the 'morning-after pill' was created, women had taken steps to make sure that the coital act did not result in pregnancy by using douches or sponges soaked in whatever was considered at the time as being the best mixture to act as an anti-spermicidal agent. Right up to the late 1940s many women were also using Rendells suppositories, which consisted of a mixture of quinine and cocoa-nut butter.

The Family Planning Association (FPA) dated back to the 1930s when five different groups amalgamated with the express aim 'that married people may space or limit their families and thus might mitigate the evils of ill health and poverty'. This was a worrying social problem: too many extra-large families needed handouts from the Poor Law Guardians, overcrowded housing led to neglect and the spread of disease, while producing a child almost annually often led to the severe breakdown in the health of thousands of women. Add to them all those who died

Once the financial situation improved and a settled home was secured, the nesting instinct took hold . . .

in childbirth or from botched backstreet abortions and the country was presented with caring for all the orphaned families who had to be taken into the workhouse or children's homes.

The FPA offered advice to married women who were then mainly fitted with the internal device known as the diaphragm or Dutch cap. However, right up to the end of the 1940s the services of the FPA were available only to married couples. Then, in 1950, a concession was made for couples about to marry. To receive help before the actual wedding day, the bride-to-be had to turn up at one of the FPA clinics armed with a letter from either her doctor or the officiating vicar to verify that she really was about to become a married woman. Later during the 1950s, trials were begun on the contraceptive pill but even when the pill went into production it was, of course, only available on prescription from the doctor – for married women. The so-called age of sexual liberation had still to dawn.

The 1950s couples who had strong religious beliefs practised what was known as the rhythm method or

natural contraception, which entailed knowing exactly at what stage of the woman's menstrual cycle she was likely to be less fertile and therefore when it was 'safe' to have intercourse. For the couple trying to have a baby, this method worked in reverse, intercourse taking place when the woman was most fertile. Most of the contributors to this work had babies within the first year to eighteen months of their marriage, which suggests that they had been reluctant to seek outside advice on contraception.

Overall, most couples had their first child within three years, even those who had delayed starting a family because they were in one of the professions such as teaching or nursing where they were expected to continue with their careers, or they needed to work in order to help support their husbands who were studying to increase their own career prospects. Once the financial situation improved and a settled home was secured, the nesting instinct took hold and then the 1950s housewife prepared for the next big challenge in her life, that of becoming a mother and bringing up a baby in the 1950s.

Sources

The Festival of Britain Guide.

Practical Cookery for All (Odhams Press, 1953 – illustrations taken from the book).

Good Housekeeping's Popular Cookery (The National Magazine Company, 1949).

Woman's Weekly, April 1959.

Stitchcraft, July 1950, July 1951–January 1959.

Colin Raistrick, archivist of Proctor & Gamble (Advertisements for Tampax reproduced by kind permission of Proctor & Gamble.)

'Divorce in England, 1950–2000: A Moral Tale', Paper by Carol Smart, 29 October 1990.

Chapter 13 quotation from the Royal Commission on Marriage and Divorce, 1956.

'The Story of a Supermarket' – the Sainsbury's Archive at the Museum of London website.

'Utility Furniture and Household Furnishings' – Board of Trade Leaflet UFD/6.

A wedding notebook of furniture, presents, etc., 1956 (unpublished).